Marion Ames Taggart

By Branscome river [electronic resource]

Marion Ames Taggart

By Branscome river [electronic resource]

ISBN/EAN: 9783741183089

Manufactured in Europe, USA, Canada, Australia, Japa

Cover: Foto ©Andreas Hilbeck / pixelio.de

Manufactured and distributed by brebook publishing software (www.brebook.com)

Marion Ames Taggart

By Branscome river [electronic resource]

"His long, strong arms quickly rescued poor Phil from his plight."—*See page* 119.

BY BRANSCOME RIVER.

BY

MARION AMES TAGGART,

Author of "Blissylvania Post-Office," "Three Girls and Especially One," etc.

NEW YORK, CINCINNATI, CHICAGO:
BENZIGER BROTHERS.

COPYRIGHT, 1897, BY BENZIGER BROTHERS

Printed in the United States of America

CONTENTS.

CHAPTER I.
Miss Keturah's Discovery, ... 7

CHAPTER II.
At the House on the Hill, ... 20

CHAPTER III.
The Boys at Stony Brook Farm, . . . 34

CHAPTER IV.
Stolen Delights, ... 48

CHAPTER V.
Silent Phil, ... 61

CHAPTER VI.
Miss Keturah's Niece, ... 76

CHAPTER VII.
Phil's Treasures, ... 98

CHAPTER VIII.
Good for Evil, ...

CHAPTER IX.
Phil Gets Acquainted, . . .

CHAPTER X.
Into the Sunset, ...

CHAPTER XI.
Good-by, Jim, ...

BY BRANSCOME RIVER.

CHAPTER I.

MISS KETURAH'S DISCOVERY.

NOTHING was farther from Miss Keturah Flint's thoughts, as she stood looking down at the foot of her hayrick in the north meadow, than Mother Goose. It never occurred to her to quote to herself:

> "Little Boy Blue, come blow your horn,
> The sheep's in the meadow, the cow's in the corn;
> Is this the way you mind your sheep,
> Under the haystack fast asleep?"

This was not merely because there were two little boys under her haystack fast asleep, but because no nursery rhymes, nor indeed rhymes of any sort, were the habit of her thought.

What she did say was, briefly: "Tramps!" What she saw was a little pale-faced boy, of about eight years, asleep in the arms of another, perhaps four years older, while a rough-coated, thin terrier, with his no-particular-colored hair matted with burs, kept guard with one eye open and one ear cocked, as he half-dozed beside the children.

Miss Keturah saw that all three small vagrants looked half-starved, and the boys' clothes were tattered; but they were certainly very clean, and there was a look of honesty on the elder lad's freckled face which she had keen enough business instinct to estimate at its full value.

"Humph! Look's if he might do," she muttered. "'Pears to be strong-bodied. I've got to get a hand somewheres. The parish could take the little one."

The small dog had endured her inspection with low growls of disapproval, but his patience gave out when she began to mutter over them. He sat up straight, and expressed his opinion of such conduct in short, sharp barks which aroused the sleepers. The elder boy opened a pair of clear gray eyes, and looked calmly and steadily up into the sharp face above him; but the younger waked with a start, and threw his arm out before his eyes with a gesture of self-defence, eloquent of many painful previous awakings.

"Where'd you come from, and what you doing sleeping in my meadow?" demanded Miss Keturah.

The boys rose to a sitting position, the elder still keeping one arm around the younger.

"Nothing; that's all—just sleeping in your meadow," he replied.

"H'm! I s'pose you know people's meadows ain't tramp lodging-houses," remarked Miss Keturah. "Where'd you come from, what's your name, and where you going to?"

The boy arose to his feet. "My name is

Jim Upper, and this is my brother Phil," he said. "We came here from New York, and we're going wherever I can find some work to take care of Phil."

"Run away from home?" asked Miss Keturah severely. "Where's your folks?"

"No, ma'am, we didn't run away from home," answered Jim emphatically. "We haven't any folks. My mother came to this country when my father died and Phil was a baby. She had a brother here, and mother thought to find him, but she never did; so she worked day and night on slop-work, sewing for the shops, till a year ago she died. And since then we've had some pretty hard luck, and we've been treated bad. So we thought we'd go into the country, and see if I couldn't get a job, and Phil might get stronger. So we came, Phil and Rags and me, and here we are, and that's all."

Rags wagged his tail at the mention of his name, as if to corroborate the story, and Miss

Keturah looked thoughtful. She surveyed Jim a few moments, and felt the muscle of his right arm in silence.

"I'll be going on," said Jim at last, making a move to start.

"No," said Miss Keturah, "stay where you are. I've been thinking. Do you steal? or drink? or smoke? or swear?"

Jim shook his head at each question.

"Well, I need a hand to work on the farm this summer," said Miss Keturah. "I've a mind to try you. You can stay here and work for your board all summer if you behave yourself."

Jim flushed with pleasure. "Thank you, ma'am," he said, feeling that he had been wrong in judging the severity of Miss Keturah's countenance. "Phil, thank the lady for taking us in."

"Hold on," said Miss Keturah. "The little fellow and the dog can't stay. I'll keep you, because I want some one, and it's hard getting help up here in haying-time, but the other boy must go to the parish."

Jim looked at her gravely, while Phil clasped his hands imploringly. The clear gray eyes were naturally pretty keen, and their powers of observation had been heightened by bitter poverty and cruel experience. Jim saw his advantage, and used it. "No, ma'am," he said quite firmly, and not as though he had no idea where he could get his supper. "No, ma'am, I won't make that bargain. I could have had a nice place in New York, but I wouldn't leave Phil and Rags. You see, mother left Phil in my care, and he'd pretty near die without me. And Rags is the only real friend I ever had, and we'll stick together through thick and thin. He never left me, and I won't leave him; eh, Rags?"

The dog gave an ecstatic yelp in response to this appeal.

"Well, suit yourself," said Miss Keturah

shortly. "You don't know when you're well off."

"I know when I ain't, and that's now," said Jim, with a frank laugh. "Look here, ma'am, I'm going on thirteen, and I can do 'most as much as a man, 'cause I'm well, and I'm used to working. Now if you got a man you'd have to pay him more wages than Phil's keep would cost, and board him, too. Phil's such a quiet little chap he'd never bother anybody, and he's real handy doing little things, while Rags would be around the farm with me all day, and you'd never miss the bone he'd have at night. I'll stay, and I'll work hard for you, and I won't ask any wages if you'll give us three board; and if you don't, I won't, and that's all about it."

Miss Keturah Flint knew as she watched the boy's steady eyes that she would get the best of the bargain, and besides the hay was ready to mow, and she was short-handed.

There was really no choice; if the boy would work at all she must have him, for it was nearly as hard to get "help" in Branscome as it was to gather oysters on the pea-vines. She resolved to close with Jim's offer, though to do so with no appearance of being beaten was difficult.

"Well," she said, "I s'pose I might as well let the boy stay, if you're so set on it. The Good Book says we must cherish the orphans and fatherless, so I expect it will all come back to me if I take the boy in. But you better remember all you owe me, and work hard to make it up. You better be spry and honest, and no lazing around. I declare, the worst of having a boy around is they're all so dreadful fond of shirking. You have to have a man for every boy, to watch him and see he's tending to business. Now if I let your brother and your dog stay here, I want you should do your best to show your gratitude."

"All right," said Jim briskly, not seeming much impressed by the charity which he could not help seeing was selfishness. "I'll do right by you, ma'am; and I don't care much about myself, for I can get along, only I do hope you'll look after Phil for me; he's not too strong," and the boy eyed his little brother anxiously. "Do you like boys, ma'am? Have you any of your own?"

"No, I can't say I do like boys," replied Miss Keturah. "And I haven't any of my own, nor any husband. I'm Miss Flint, and I own this farm of a hundred acres, and it's just as well run as any in the country. Keturah Flint was I born, and Keturah Flint will I die, and no thanks to anybody if I'm rich, and no husband and boys to make me poor."

"Well, you'll be good to Phil, won't you, ma'am?" Jim persisted.

"I'll treat him as I think right, young man," said Miss Keturah. "I'm not going to let him sleep in the best bedroom, and I don't know as I shall make him mince pies for his dinner; he'll be a charity boy, and I shall treat him according. But I guess he'll make out; and don't you get saucy, or I'll send you both to the right-about-face. I suppose I've got to look up some decent clothes for you, but I guess I can get some blue jean down to the village. If you want to come along with me to the house, I'll let you see where I'll put you to sleep, and you can begin by helping with the cows to-night. Ever milk?"

"No, ma'am, there are no cows in New York, except a queer kind in the Zoo," said Jim. "But I'll learn."

"Yes, I expect I'll have to teach you everything, and it'll be more'n you're worth, not to mention the keep of the boy and the dog. Howsomever, a bargain's a bargain, and ours is made; come along now." So saying, Miss Keturah led the way across the soft grass like a grenadier, and the three strangers followed with doubting hearts. Jim feared for Phil, Phil feared for both, and Rags' disapproval of Miss Keturah's manner was shown by the alertness of his air and the closeness with which he stuck to Phil's side.

Miss Keturah led them to a rough chamber in the barn, over the carriage-room. The rafters were unfinished, but the air was fragrant with hay, and Jim liked the independence and feeling of camping out that struck him on entering. But Phil cried out in horror: "Oh, the rat, the rat!" and shrank back in terror; while Rags, springing forward, had the rat fast before he had time to scuttle into his hole, and with one shake laid him dead at Jim's feet.

"Now that's a smart dog!" exclaimed Miss Keturah in involuntary admiration.

"I tell you he is," said Jim proudly. "There isn't a dog anywhere round can beat Rags at rat-catching. You won't have any rats this summer if you'll let Rags go around."

"But what kind of silly sissy behavior do you call this?" added Miss Keturah, turning to where Phil stood shaking in nervous tremor. "Now if you're going to be such a Miss Nancy as this you'd better go along, for boys are bad enough, but a boy that's a girl is no earthly good."

"He'll get over that," said Jim hastily. "Phil's not strong, and he's had a hard time since mother died, and he's been hungry ever so long. He'll be all right when he gets stronger."

"Well, see you're not so silly," said Miss Keturah. "I'll have you a bed made here, and I'll put a chair in maybe, and you can wash at the pump in the yard. We have supper pretty soon now, and when you hear a bell ring you go into the house round the back way." And Miss Keturah disappeared down the stairs.

"See, Phil, we can see the river out this window." said Jim gently, putting his arm around the little boy, and leading him to look out on the beautiful country view spread before them. "Rags won't let any rats come, and we'll be cozy here. You'll like to live in this pretty place all summer, won't you?"

"It's lovely, Jim, and the river sings so nice I'll love to lie by it, if she'll let me," said Phil; "but I'm afraid of her, Jim. But we are all together, and I'll be happy. I was so afraid she'd make us leave each other."

"Nobody can do that, Phil boy," said Jim, hugging him fiercely. "I'm going to work for a home for you, and I'd like to see any one part us."

CHAPTER II.

AT THE HOUSE ON THE HILL.

"Come on, Carl; are you ready?" said the girl.

"All ready, Carol; only lend a hand to put the box on the wagon," answered the boy.

Each child took an end of the soap-box that stood on the grass, and lifted it solemnly on the express-wagon waiting close by.

"Why, you aren't ready at all, Carl Blake," said Carola. "You haven't on your vestments."

"Well, that's because I am the undertaker now; we always had some one with us before to be undertaker, but as there's nobody here to-day I've got to be undertaker till we get to the cemetery, and then I'll be priest—the vestments are in the front of the wagon," said Carl. "Get behind, Carola, and cry. You must cry hard, because there's no one else to mourn for him. Got your handkerchief?"

"Yes," responded Carola, taking her place behind the wagon, and burying her face in the handkerchief, spread very large for the office of chief mourner. Then the funeral procession started down towards the foot of the garden, where the cemetery lay, while Carl chanted to a very minor air of their own invention the following stanza from "Through the Looking-glass," which had been adopted as the funeral dirge:

> "'I weep for you,' the Walrus said,
> 'I deeply sympathize.'
> With sobs and tears he sorted out
> Those of the largest size,
> Holding his pocket-handkerchief
> Before his streaming eyes."

This, from the time they were five years old, had been the invariable order of proceeding for the Blake twins at the obsequies of their pets. No two children ever were more undivided in taste and possessions, from their hearts and names, which were one, to the smallest trifle, than were the Blake twins; and through the long summers which they spent at Branscome, in the house on the hill which had been their grandfather's, they played together in unwearied pleasure in each other's society, of which school partly deprived them in winter.

Carl and Carola both loved animals dearly, and had a perpetual succession of pets, some of which dying, as pets, alas! too often will, had been buried in a portion of ground at the foot of the garden, which they called the cemetery. Here, as summers passed, many little graves were made, for Carl and Carola were eleven, and for six years had been sadly laying away their four-footed friends.

To-day's funeral called forth no anguish, for it was that of a red fox shot in an attempt on the chicken-coop. The twins had interfered to save his body from being ignominiously cast out, for, as they justly said, he was neither to blame for being a fox nor for liking chickens, as they themselves did. So they secured Reynard's body, put it decently in a soap-box, and were burying it according to their usual rites, with his name and the cause and date of his death inscribed in india-ink on the box-cover. Still, though they resolved to treat him with kindly respect, they could not mourn for the fox deeply, and hence Carola's sobs were so regular as to arouse a suspicion of their sincerity, and Carl chanted louder and more slowly than usual to cover the lack of the trembling which overcame his voice when he sang the dirge at the funeral of a beloved kitten or lamented puppy.

When the funeral procession of the late fox arrived at the boundary of the little cemetery it paused, and Carl and Carola lifted the box from the wagon, and carried it solemnly to the grave which Carl had previously dug. Here it was deposited, while Carl took his vestments from the wagon, and prepared to transform himself from the undertaker into the priest. First he put on an old black skirt of his mother's to represent the cassock. Then, with Carola's help and many pins, a white table-cloth was fastened over his shoulders in such wise as to look not unlike a surplice, and a black ribbon represented the stole. The clerical dignity was impaired by the difficulty with which Carl sought the matches which he had forgotten to take out of the pocket of his knickerbockers when he put on his vestments; but finally they were produced, and the four candles lighted which were to stand at each side of the soap-box casket.

"Now then," said Carl, "take your place."

Carola obediently stood at the foot of the box, while Carl took up his stand at the head.

At every funeral Carl preached a sermon, and each sermon began with the same words: "My brethren, it is not usual for Catholics to preach a funeral sermon, but in this case I feel that one is deserved." Then the preacher proceeded to set forth as eloquently as he could the virtues of the departed, and the lesson to be derived from his death. To-day Carl related in such touching words how the fox had died while trying to get food for his wife and children that Carola was moved to real tears, and he ended his discourse by bidding his hearers imitate Mr. Fox's noble example, and be always ready to lay down their lives for those they loved.

After this the box was sprinkled three times with pure water, and the children recited in alternation, like a versicle and response, first Longfellow's "Psalm of Life," and then "The Burial of Sir John Moore," which if not wholly appropriate, yet were solemn and made a dignified substitute for psalms which they dared not use because it would be irreverent. This ended the funeral services, and the box was lowered into the grave which Carola helped Carl fill up, and the funeral was over. But before leaving the cemetery the twins had to arrange flowers on the graves of all their pets, each one of which had a tombstone at its head, behind which was a bottle to hold the flowers.

There were the graves of three rabbits which had been Carl's, and of a tiny monkey from Brazil who had died of inflammation of the lungs in the more severe northern climate, having made life a burden to the family for six months by his tricks. There were two canary-birds, a tame chicken, a puppy, and a big St. Bernard, who had died of old age, and several kittens, last but not least of which was dear little Tig—short for Tiger —the kitten which Carola had found when he was too small to eat, and who had been nourished by means of a rag dipped in milk till he could eat like other catkins. Tig had grown up to be devoted to his little foster-mother, and submitted patiently to her dressing him in her doll's clothes, and taking him for long rides in her doll-carriage, laid on his back, with his paws drooping over the carriage-strap. He had died of sore throat; and just before he died, hearing his beloved little mistress' voice, he had dragged his poor little body to her feet, and tried to lick them, raising his already blind eyes to her face.

Each pet had its own gravestone; but Tig, the dearest of all, alone had a poetical epitaph, composed amid bitter tears by Carola, and which ran thus:

> "Here lies our little boy;
> O'er him we weep;
> When alive he was our joy,
> But now he's gone to sleep."

"I think we would better put a slate stone at the head of the fox's grave, Carol," said Carl. "And I'll draw a hen on it, and we'll write: 'Died for dinner.'"

"Then they won't know whether the fox was eaten or not," objected Carola. "That sounds as though some one had him for dinner. I say just write : 'Here lies Mr. Reynard Fox. Died June 20th, 1896. Thou shalt not steal.'"

"That isn't fair," said Carl decidedly. "I say don't have anything against him on his tombstone. I don't see why he shouldn't like chickens as well as we. Let's just say : 'He did his best.'"

In the mean time a tall, gaunt woman had come into the garden through the rear gate, unseen by the children. The house on the hill, "the big house" as it was called, was not much visited by the people in the village. The Blakes were only there in the summer, and there were few bonds between them and the natives of Branscome. Mrs. Blake's grandfather had built the house, but she had never known it except as a summer home. The Branscome folk had been shocked when the granddaughter of "the old squire," as they called him, had become a Catholic, and later married one of her own faith; but New England prejudices against religion are not as strong as the prejudice in favor of money, and as the Blakes had a good share of wealth they were looked up to as the great family of Branscome.

The woman who had come into the garden paused to look with amazement on the scene in the cemetery, where the four candles stuck in the ground were burning low, and Carl, still attired in his funny imitation of a priest's vestments, was gravely helping Carola arrange the flowers in the bottles.

"For the land's sake!" she exclaimed at last.

The children turned at the sound, and saw her for the first time.

"How do you do, Miss Flint?" they both said as if they were doing nothing unusual. "Did you come to see mamma?"

"Yes, I did," gasped Miss Flint, wondering whether the Blake twins were at all "touched in their minds."

"If you can just wait one moment till we finish putting these flowers on the graves, we'll go with you to the house," said Carl. "Or if you're in a hurry, you can go right on through the garden."

"I'll wait," said Miss Keturah briefly.

"There," sighed Carola finally as she arose, having fastened the last bottle back in its place behind the monkey's tombstone. "Now we're ready, Miss Flint."

Taking up the tongue of the wagon, they preceded her up the path, she following in profound astonishment and equal disapproval.

"Mamma, here's Miss Flint," cried Carl, leading the way to where his mother sat on the big piazza.

"Take this rocking-chair, Miss Flint," said Mrs. Blake, as her guest seated herself rigidly on the stiffest chair on the piazza.

"No, I thank you; I don't care about lolling much," responded Miss Keturah. "I come to tell you about a boy, two boys, I've got down to my house. I found 'em yest'day asleep in my meadow. They were poor, and hadn't any home, and I've taken 'em in for the summer."

"That was very good of you, Miss Flint," said Mrs. Blake, inwardly wondering.

"Well, the youngest is peakéd and only eight, but the other's over twelve and pretty rugged. I calc'late he'll work on the farm for their keep," responded Miss Flint. "What I come to you about is this. These boys are Catholics, and nothing'll do but they must walk over to North Branscome to church to-morrow, or at least the oldest one; I d' know but it's too far for the little one to do it. If they'd go to our meeting I'd get some Sunday clothes for 'em down to our Dorcas society; but I thought if they're goin' to yours, maybe your folks could help clothe 'em."

"Certainly, Miss Flint. Very likely I have something of Carl's that would do for part of their wardrobe, and I should be very glad to get whatever else they needed. It is very good of you to help them get to church," said Mrs. Blake, marvelling at such liberality in Miss Keturah Flint of all people.

"Well, I s'pose you can't force folks to your own meeting," said Miss Keturah, not saying that she had tried, and that Jim had told her that he had promised his dead mother to go to Mass regularly, and see that Phil also did, and that he would stay nowhere that he could not fulfil this promise, whereupon, having already found him very useful, she had yielded with bad grace.

"But, Miss Flint, it is seven or eight miles to North Branscome and back," said Mrs. Blake, rising. "That is too far for children to walk in the hot summer sunshine. You send the two little boys here at half-past nine, and I'll try to smuggle them into a corner of my servants' carriage, which is big enough for one or two more."

"Very well, Mrs. Blake, I'll tell 'em," said Miss Keturah, reflecting that this arrangement would leave Jim less tired for Monday morning.

"And now if you will come with me, I will see what Carl can spare for your little waifs," added Mrs. Blake.

"A boy at Stony Brook Farm!" exclaimed Carl, as Miss Flint and his mother disappeared. "My! I don't envy him. I wonder what he's like."

"I don't know; we'll see to-morrow," said Carola.

CHAPTER III.

THE BOYS AT STONY BROOK FARM.

PROMPTLY at half-past nine two small figures entered the gate of the "house on the hill." Carl and Carola, standing on the piazza, looked at them with interest. To the smaller of the two Carola, in her white dress, with her dark curls and soft brown eyes, appeared like a vision of some fairer world, a part of the beauty of the wild roses, and grass, and trees, and sky, and singing birds for the first time delighting his childish eyes, used only to the ugly sights and sounds of poverty in the city. The elder boy felt more interest in Carl, who repeated in a boyish form Carola's beauty, and, Jim thought, looked to be a first-rate fellow. When they arrived at the foot of the steps the four children stared at each other a moment or two, Phil hanging back shyly, till the ice was broken by Carl demanding suddenly: "Did you cut that basket?" pointing to a small basket carved from a peach-stone which hung on a string across the front of his jacket, after the manner of a watch-guard.

"Yes," said Jim, his face lighting up with a laugh. "Suppose you think it's a queer thing to wear," and he began to push it along the string with the intention of concealing it in a pocket.

"No, I don't; don't do that," cried Carl, springing down the steps. "Here, let me look at it. It's fine; come see, Carol." Carola descended a little timidly, but grew enthusiastic over the basket, and especially over the skill with which a tiny ornament was cut where the handles began.

"Do you like it, honest?" asked Jim. "Pooh! 'tisn't much; I can cut heaps better than that. If I had some walnut-shells I'd show you a basket! And I'd cut one for you too that would hold a thimble," he added, looking at Carola admiringly.

"Oh! thank you; I'd love to have one," she cried; while Carl said: "I can get all the walnuts you want. If I bring them down to the farm, will you cut them?"

"She won't let me have a minute long enough to cut a slice of bread, hardly," said Jim with a funny grimace, jerking his head over his shoulder towards the direction in which he had come. "But I'll tell you what: if you'll bring the walnuts down to the meadow where the cows are at the time I have to go after them to bring them home, I'll see if I can stay a few minutes and begin one anyway."

"It must be pretty tough working for Miss Keturah," Carl began; but before he could get farther, or Jim reply, the carriages came around from the stable, and Mr. and Mrs.

Blake and the servants came out, and it was time to start for church.

"Say, ask them to let you get down, and walk through the woods," said Carl. "Carola and I always do; we start early purposely that we may have time to walk there; it's lovely. We call it 'Angels' Hush'—Carola named it—it's so still and sort of peaceful there."

Jim promised this readily, and he and Phil were squeezed into the big carriage that held the servants, while the Blakes got into the small carriage with their father and mother, and the pleasant little journey to North Branscome began.

To Phil, on his knees between the legs of kind Matt, the coachman, with his chin on the dashboard, this, his first drive, was such bliss that it seemed it must be a dream, and he scarcely dared breathe, lest he should wake himself, and find horses, motion, soft June air, and song of birds all vanished.

At the edge of the woods the small carriage stopped, and Carl and Carola got down, and signalled impatiently to Matt to come up, and stop to allow Jim and Phil to do the same. Carl began where they had left off without loss of time. "How do you stand it at Miss Keturah's? isn't she a terror?" he asked.

"Well, I should say!" said Jim emphatically. "She's like that big steam-mower she's got; she swoops down on everything she goes by. I get on, because I don't mind much though she makes me work like time, and I'm not used to farmwork. But I'm 'most afraid for Phil. You see," Jim went on, lowering his voice as he and Carl walked a little faster ahead of the other two, "Phil doesn't like to be treated rough; he's a queer little chap, and I'm awful afraid she'll be rough to him. Mother told me to look after him, and I'm doing my best; but you see it's kind of hard to earn enough to take care of us both till I get bigger, and we haven't any home, so

I thought I'd better try staying here if we could. The only thing is she's hard up for help on the farm, and she can't afford to lose me, and I know, if I do say it, that I've done a lot of work for a boy these days since I came. So if she gets too smart I'll tell her I'll leave, and I guess I can manage her that way. We had a fight about going to Mass, and I came out on top that day. She said she wouldn't have me going to the Catholic church, and I'd got to go down to her meeting-house here and be taught the Gospel. But I told her I'd promised my mother I'd be a Catholic, and see Phil was one, and I was going to Mass every Sunday, even if it was as far as she said, and if she tried to stop me I'd leave. I said I guessed there was some other farm that was short of hands besides hers, and I'd find it. So the old lady came down, but she was as mad as a snapping-turtle, and she's been reading me tracts every night before I go to bed ever since, and she had fish on Thursday, and a pretty decent meat dinner for Stony Brook Farm on Friday."

Carl laughed; he had always been called a great talker, but he found the new boy "could talk all round him," as he told his father when he got back into the carriage.

"Did you come from New York? We live in New York winters," Carl said.

"Yes," replied Jim.

"Where did you live? I live near the Cathedral," said Carl.

Jim gave him a quizzical look. "That's the east side," he said. "We never lived on the east side; it's not genteel, though I know the Vanderbilts and those people live around there. No, sir; I lived in the Thirty streets —we moved into two or three of 'em over near the North River."

"My! isn't that——" Carl began, but stopped himself before he said more.

"Yes, it is, if you mean isn't that a pretty queer neighborhood," Jim said coolly. "But you see we were awful poor, and my mother killed herself trying to earn enough to live even as poor as that."

"But you don't talk——" Carl began again, and a second time remembered in time to stop.

"Don't talk like a tenement-house tough," said Jim good-naturedly. "Well, you see my mother was pretty nice, about as nice as she could be, and was well educated, and she tried her very best to keep us decent, and a fellow who had such a mother as she was had to try to be decent to please her; you couldn't help it. So I never had much to say to the boys in the row, and they used to call me 'dude,' and 'Chauncey Depew,' and things like that, till I blacked their eyes for them, and then they didn't dare holler unless they were across the street."

While this conversation was going on, Carola, walking behind with Phil, found her companion very different. Not a word would Phil say, but not a fern, or blossom, or twitter of bird seemed to escape his quick eye and ear, and he listened with evident delight to all that Carola told him of the new life around him. The little girl had received that best of all educations, knowledge of the secrets of nature; for, since they had been almost babies, the twins had been taken for long, blissful tramps in fields and woods with their father, who had taught them to see and know the loveliness that so many big and little folk pass unheeding. So Carola could tell Phil such wonderful things of why the little birches quivered all the time, as if forever applauding the birds' concerts, and how this bird built its nest, or that little insect kept alive a whole family of plants, or how the rock they passed got those scratches when the icebergs went crashing down to the sea through this valley long ages ago, that Phil regarded her as a marvel of learning, and these stories as a new sort of fairy tale more enchanting than all the wonders that could be invented.

Carl, swinging a lithe stick as he walked ahead, cut off the head of a nodding daisy that grew in a sunny spot made by an opening of the woods along the roadside.

Phil turned back, and picked up the bright little head, and laying it in the palm of one hand, stroked it gently with the other. "Poor daisy! I'll take care of you," he whispered.

"Now that's just the way I feel," cried Carola eagerly. "It would seem like being cruel to leave it in the dirt, wouldn't it?"

Phil nodded. "It looks like you," he said shyly.

"Like me!" exclaimed Carola. "Why does it?"

"I don't know; it's so white and pretty," said Phil. Little Phil had never in his short life heard of the great German poet Heine, yet the child and the poet had the same thought, for Heine too had said:

"Oh, thou art like a flower."

"We'll come down to the meadow at six," said Carl, as they drew near Stony Brook Farm, where Jim and Phil were to be set down. "And I'll bring some walnuts, and you can show me how to make the baskets."

"All right," said Jim, "if I can get time. Anyway you bring the walnuts, and if I can't stop to-night I'll make some baskets for you when I do get a chance. I'm ever so much obliged for taking us to church; and Phil looks better for the drive," he added, taking off his cap to Mrs. Blake. "Phil, say 'Thank you.'"

"Thank you," said Phil, in a tiny voice, trying to get behind his brother.

"That boy has gentle blood, I am sure," said Mrs. Blake as they drove away.

Her husband laughed. "Gentle blood behaves very roughly sometimes, my dear, and rough blood very gently," he said. "It is hard telling. One thing is certain: he has picked up some gentle manners."

Miss Keturah, divided in her mind between pleasure in having the children living under her roof brought home by "the hill folks," and disgust in being outgeneralled in the matter of going to church, was found by Jim and Phil on their return in an uncertain temper, which generally means, as in her case, a very certain bad temper. She compelled the boys to learn a whole chapter of the Old Testament and one of the psalms that afternoon, and succeeded in taking every bit of the beauty from the Hebrew poet's words by associating them in the minds of both boys with her harsh nasal tones.

It was a little later than usual when they went for the cows, and Jim was so angry that he did not see the beauty of the hour. But Phil straightway forgot all earthly troubles, and walked up the hill in the blaze of the

June sunset in a maze of delight. They found the twins awaiting them, well supplied with English walnuts; but there was no time to make baskets, and Jim and Carl fell to plotting how they should outwit Miss Keturah, and go fishing in the tempting river that flowed through Branscome. Phil plucked a bunch of wild rosebuds and gave them to Carola. The smell of sweet clover and new-mown hay was in the air; the cows, with their sweet breath and fresh, milky smell, went swinging along, the sunshine resting on their glossy dun flanks; and the blazing west made the whole earth radiant till the stars should come.

Carl's and Jim's voices rose and fell energetically, but Carola and Phil were silent. Presently Phil slipped one little hand into Carola's. "I wish mamma could see it," he said, and his voice quivered.

"It's nicer where she is," returned Carola softly, "and she's glad you can have this."

"So am I," said Phil, and there was no cruelty, nor poverty, nor Miss Keturah in the world that moment for one of the boys at Stony Brook Farm.

CHAPTER IV.

STOLEN DELIGHTS.

IN spite of the obstacles to the friendship between Jim and Carl, or rather perhaps because of them, it grew and flourished. It is in human nature to value most that for which we have to struggle most to attain, and Romeo and Juliet hardly had to make more effort to meet than did these two boys. Miss Keturah managed to keep nearly every moment of Jim's time occupied; and if ever he did have a moment's leisure, she felt such strong objections to people being happy in their own way that she would be sure to refuse consent to almost any request that Jim might frame. But it is difficult to prevent two bright boys from having a little fun together if their hearts are set upon it, and these two did manage to squeeze out some moments of joy, the sweeter for being stolen. Carl got into the way of rising early, and meeting Jim when he and Rags took the cows to pasture, and at night when the cows came home, Carola and Phil would be added to the other three, and the daily walks through the dewy, grass-grown roads were an unspeakable delight to all five.

Although the twins had been born and had always lived in New York, they found that they knew nothing of their own city as compared with the stories of life there which Jim had to tell. For when had they ever visited dime museums on the Bowery, and what glory had ever befallen them such as Jim could boast, who knew a youth of eighteen who was frequently taken into the service of a down-town theatre to serve as one of the twelve men who represented the army in the play, or the crowd on the city streets, according to the melodrama being enacted?

Glimpses of such an interesting world as this Jim gave them in the talks which they snatched from the very horns of Miss Keturah's cows—to speak figuratively—and in return they unconsciously imparted to Jim fragments of knowledge of which he had been deprived, and to which he took so kindly as to confirm Mrs. Blake's belief in his having inherited gentle tastes.

Then there were the drives every Sunday to North Branscome to Mass, and the loitering walks through the woods to which all four looked forward longingly all the week, and of which at last even Rags was not deprived, for he was such a clever little dog that there was no trouble in making him understand that he must stay in the carriage during Mass, and so there could be no objection to his trotting to North Branscome under the carriage, which he did henceforth with the utmost pleasure.

But best of all was the glorious day when

Miss Keturah commissioned Jim to take Jenny, the old mare, and drive to the village to fulfil certain duties for her there; for, having performed this feat successfully the first time, he was allowed to go frequently, and Phil and Rags accompanied him as a matter of course. It would have been a duller boy than Jim who had not found a way to pick up Carl and Carola on these trips, and the five friends—counting Rags—made the most of these opportunities. Now a slower beast than Jenny would have been hard to find; Jim said he had seen trained seals in the dime museums "wobble around faster than she could trot;" but although the Blake twins generally rode behind their father's fast chestnuts, they hailed a drive with Jim to the village behind Jenny with rapture that a drive behind the livelier team could never waken. For while old Jenny swung along at the pace which she considered fitting to her age and dignity, all the while slapping her flanks with her scrubby tail, and covering the children with her white hairs, because, as Carola remarked, she "shed her feathers all the year round," Jim would give the reins to Phil, who loved to drive, and sitting on the edge of the seat, with his elbows on his knees, would give imitations of the men on the farm, or the group in the grocery store, or even the awful Miss Keturah herself, till the children were in convulsions of laughter, for Jim was a born mimic.

But blissful as these opportunities of meeting were, they were brief, and Jim and Carl still sighed for a whole day of fishing. They had counted on having this on the Fourth of July; but when Jim had asked about it, Miss Keturah had sniffed contemptuously. "Holiday!" she said. "I guess not. I'd like to know if we're to stop work, and let the whole farm go to rack and ruin just because our forefathers tended to their business and set the country free! No, young man; you just put such notions straight out of your head. It's enough for us that there was a Fourth of July, and we're free to work for ourselves, and ain't paying taxes to a tyrant, without making it an excuse to quit work and loaf the day away."

Jim did not see this, and felt injured, for he had worked hard and faithfully, and, like most of us, considered himself entitled to some reward for unflagging virtue. So, as he told Carl afterwards, on the following Saturday he "struck."

"See here, Miss Flint," he said, facing her squarely, "I'm not going to learn psalms for you to-morrow nor one more Sunday afternoon. I've a right to some time to myself, and I'm going to have it. I have to come back Sunday noon to fodder down the horses, and change the cows into the other pasture, but I'm going to take my Sunday afternoon for myself, and Phil's coming with me."

"Don't you sauce me," said Miss Keturah.

recovering her breath after this audacity. "You're goin' to do just what I tell you."

"I don't want to sauce you," retorted Jim, "but I've got to have a day of rest, and Sunday's for us all. I'll keep my word, and do all your work, but I won't learn psalms and the things you want me to learn, because it doesn't rest me."

Miss Keturah recognized the determination which she had encountered before in her young assistant, who had become so important to her that she deemed it better to capitulate. "I sh'd think you'd be ashamed of yourself, not liking to learn godliness. Do you know where you'll go to?" she said sternly.

"Yes, ma'am; I'll go to the woods," said Jim with a twinkle. "I'm going to church all right, and I'd like to learn to be good; but it doesn't make me good to stay in all of the only afternoon I've got, having you teach me things out of that awful book that you read me last Sunday. No, sir, Miss Flint, I'm going to take Phil and Rags, and we'll have our Sunday afternoons to ourselves, if you don't mind."

Miss Keturah minded, but she only sniffed and turned away. "If you want to go to ruin, I d' know as I'm called upon to hinder," she said. "You're headstrong for a boy of your age, and I shan't be held responsible, for I've offered you the chance, and you love idleness better than righteousness."

"Well, I haven't been very idle so far," said Jim, laughing, for he saw that he had won the day. "I guess I don't like bad things, only there are bad ways of being good, I'm thinking."

The next afternoon Jim and Phil and Rags set forth to meet Carl and Carola, and go to a spot in the woods which Carl was to show them. Carl appeared with two fishing-poles, and Carola with a basket of sandwiches and cookies, and there was no flaw in their happiness as they walked under the great trees, the fragrant pine-needles hushing their footfalls, and the ripple of the river reaching their ears faintly, but growing louder as they neared it.

"Now here's the place," cried Carl, springing a few steps ahead of the others. "How is this?"

"Oh, my!" cried Jim, while Phil caught his breath.

A sudden turn of the path had brought them to the river, which an opening straight to its edge revealed to them. The stream made a bend at this point, and right in the elbow thus formed nestled a tiny island covered with beautiful trees to the water's edge.

"Now this is the place Carola and I love best," said Carl, looking at it with loving pride. "We've made stepping-stones over, and we take off our shoes and stockings to go across, because the stones are under water, and when we get over we play it's an enchanted island, and no one in all the world but us knows how to get on it. And we've got the nicest cubby-hole over there for a closet that you ever saw, and we keep things in it."

"What things?" asked Phil.

"Fishing-tackle, and games, and books, and such things," replied Carl. "Come on over."

They bared their feet, and started; but nervous little Phil shuddered so much at the chill of the water that Jim took him picka-back, and they proceeded thus, Rags swimming after, and having his opinion of the performance.

"I'll tell you what," said Jim, after they had reached the isle in safety, and had explored its beauties. "I'll tell you: let's rig up a drawbridge, and pull it up after us."

"How could you?" demanded Carl.

"Easy," said Jim. "You get a plank just as wide as the river here——"

"Ten feet," interrupted Carl.

"All right. You get the plank ten feet long, and I'll rig a pulley up in the highest tree, and put a rope through some staples on the end of the board, and we'll pull it up after we've walked over on it."

"Jolly, wouldn't that be fun!" cried Carl.

"Lovely!" echoed Carola, clapping her hands.

"And then we can play it's an enchanted island all the more," added Jim.

"And we'll call it Dimanche Island, because we come here Sunday afternoons," added Carola, who had begun to study French.

"Now let's fish," said Carl, who was dying to show his skill.

Jim and he each took one of Carl's poles, and rigged up a branch of a tree as a pole for Phil. Carola declined to fish, for she would not bait her own hooks, nor take off a fish if she happened to catch one, and was too firm a believer in fair play to make the rest do her work for her. She fell to weaving leaves into plates, and sweeping up the place preparatory to setting her table.

The fish were not very lively, but Jim and Carl caught a few, and were making ready to pull in, and clean the fish for frying over the faggot fire, which was part of the sport, when they discovered that Phil, the dreamer, had forgotten all about fishing in the delight of hearing the little waves lap the stones, and was sitting in blissful oblivion of all around him, with the biggest fish of the afternoon on his hook. How they laughed, and how good the fish did taste cooked by themselves, albeit they were a trifle smoked and rare!

It was the first time in all their short lives that Jim and Phil had ever enjoyed such an afternoon of real woodland joys, and they parted from the twins with rapturous promises to come every week.

Miss Keturah scolded because they were a little late bringing in the cows, but Jim and Phil went to bed perfectly happy, with a contentment nothing could mar.

CHAPTER V.

SILENT PHIL.

THE days at Stony Brook Farm were divided in Phil's mind into three parts. The first division began with their waking in the rough barn chamber and Jim's good-morning kiss, which, keeping up their mother's custom, he always gave him. This division included taking the cows to pasture, feeding the horses, pigs, chickens, and calves, and ended after their hasty breakfast when Jim went to work.

The second part of the day was not so satisfactory, for it was short, hardly going beyond the dinner-hour when Jim returned, and immediately after which he resumed labor.

The last division was the best, for it began

with the beautiful sunset walk to fetch the cows back, and only ended when he fell asleep in Jim's arms, where he always took refuge from the mysterious sounds heard in the barn at night, and which always frightened him, though he knew they were but the animals stirring in their stalls below.

Some days, to be marked in gold in the calendar, had a fourth division, when he went with Jim to watch him work, or when Jim was sent on errands where Phil could go with him.

All the rest of the day Phil did not count; he merely existed, and it was a lonely existence enough that he led, and he had no one to keep him company, for Rags went daily with Jim to the fields.

Not that Phil regretted this, for sometimes Miss Keturah boxed his ears, and he felt sure that if Rags had been about she would have struck him too; and though Phil did not like being struck himself, he could not have borne a blow on Rags. Miss Keturah was not unkind to Phil, according to her notions of kindness, but the child was so silent, so unlike what she remembered children to have been when she was a little girl and went to school—since which time she had known none—and was so dreamy, that he annoyed her, and she treated him with contemptuous harshness. Phil tried very hard to do and be what she wished, for he felt oppressed by her scorn, and in his shy, mute way longed for love from every one and everything. But somehow he never succeeded in pleasing Miss Keturah, or winning even one kindly glance from her, and at last he gave up hoping for it, and went about in silent, benumbed pain that made him more unchildlike than ever.

Out of doors alone Phil was different. All the chickens and sheep knew him and followed him, and this proof of affection made him light-hearted and playful when he was with these dumb friends. A lame hen that was of no use, and an old sheep getting blind, were his favorites, and Miss Keturah, noting it, set it down as a new proof of his lack of wit. Sometimes she caught him sitting on the broad back door-step in the sunshine, crooning to himself in queer little tunes still queerer little jingles of words, and she felt convinced that the boy was really, as she said, "a zany." One day stealing up behind him she heard him chanting:

> "God made the flowers,
> God made the sea;
> God made the sun and stars;
> God made me."

It was the child's way of trying to express the sense of God's nearness which the big and little things of His handiwork gave him; but Miss Keturah burst into a harsh laugh behind him, and Phil shrank frightened and hurt around the corner into the shadow.

Then, too, Phil was a coward, for he was afraid of people, and afraid of darkness, and afraid of he did not know what — chiefly afraid of being afraid — and Miss Keturah, who did not know what nerves meant, despised the little fellow for this weakness. However, she managed to make Phil useful in sundry small ways, and employed him to wipe dishes, and dust, and fetch and carry for her. He tried so hard to do these small offices well that it would have been pathetic if there had been any one there to see his efforts, which were more than ever likely to fail from overanxiety.

One day he was wiping dishes, and Miss Keturah was more than usually snappish, and Phil, who always shrank like a sensitive-plant at a harsh touch, went back and forth between sink and table benumbed and trembling. At this unfavorable time Neb, the cat—short for Nebuchadnezzar, as Miss Keturah would have spelled the name of the king of Babylon— Neb, walking sedately across the kitchen floor, saw fit to sit down suddenly to attend to some neglected point in his toilet, and Phil, not seeing him, tripped over him, and the dish that he was wiping flew out of his hands, and was shattered in a dozen pieces.

Miss Keturah, taking her hands from the dish-tub with a shake to free them from suds, turned to the trembling child, and struck him first on one ear and then on the other. "I'll teach you to go mooning 'round, breaking my china, you zany!" she cried. "Take that, and that!"

Although Phil's short life had been a sad one, he had never been struck, and he received the blows in an agony that held in it so much amazement as to prevent his uttering a sound. But when he had obediently picked up the pieces, and carried them out to the rubbish-heap, he met on his way back his favorite half-blind sheep, who thrust her nose confidingly into his feverish hand. The caress of poor old Nancy opened the pent-up agony of his heart; Phil put his arms around her, and, laying his face on her dingy wool, burst into such floods of tears as washed her white in one little spot, and eased the tightening pain that was choking him.

This was the first time that Miss Keturah had struck Phil, but after this the occasions came more frequently, and in a certain sense Phil grew used to the blow that always seemed to strike so far below the smarting flesh. He never told Jim; if he had, it might have been different; but, young as he was, Phil realized how hard it is to get a home and food, and he resolved not to tell Jim anything that might lead him to go away from that for which they had searched so long, or to bother Jim with trouble which was his alone. So brave little cowardly Phil kept his secret, and cried out his troubles only to old Nancy.

But Phil had one friend besides old Nancy and the lame hen who sometimes kept him company while Jim was at work, and this was Seth Peters. Seth Peters was one of the curiosities of Branscome. He seemed to most of the village children to be as old as it was possible for man to be; Phil seemed to consider him of suitable age to be a companion for a little boy of eight; in reality he was something over forty. He walked with his shoulders bent forward, and wore a gentle smile on his pale face, while his light, far-gazing eyes never seemed to look at anything nearer than the moon. Yet not the smallest blade or blossom escaped them; he spent the summer roaming the fields, gathering herbs which in winter he made up into decoctions for the cure of simple maladies, or sold dried to whoever would buy them. He was rarely known to speak, and shunned companionship, but by some unexpressed attraction and sympathy Phil and he became friends. No one knew how it began, but it soon became a custom for silent little Phil and Seth to join forces whenever a chance offered, and wander through the fields hand in hand in speechless, happy communion. Seth must have broken the silence when they were away from the village, for Phil soon acquired considerable knowledge of the plants, and of the lives of the little creatures that are to be found among them, and repeated to Jim at night bits of simple wisdom that Seth had dropped. They were a strange but not ill-assorted pair, and Phil confided to Jim that next to him and Carola Blake he loved Seth Peters, the herbman.

There was one thing in which Phil succeeded in pleasing Miss Keturah, though, true to her principle that unfailing reproof was wholesome, and praise bad for the character, she never betrayed the fact. Early and late, for pure love of the flowers, Phil weeded and worked in the garden, till Miss Keturah's beds were the envy of her neighbors. Yet, though he longed to gather some of the sweetest of the blossoms which he had so carefully tended, to carry to the little church in North Branscome for Our Lady's altar, he dared not venture to ask permission to do so, but gathered instead the rarest and sweetest wild flowers which he found in his Saturday walk with Seth.

Carola had told him that the maidenhair fern was called thus in honor of the Blessed Virgin; "maidenhair" meaning the Maiden Mary's hair, just as the French call the lily-of-the-valley "Our Lady's tears." So one Saturday Phil brought in as much as he could carry of the delicate wild maidenhair, and he and Jim tied it on a cross made of two small branches, and put it into water overnight to take to church in the morning. But the next day the sun was hot, and the way to North Branscome was long, and when they reached there the delicate ferns were drooping. Phil caught his breath in a little sob as he saw it. "Oh! I wanted to give it to the Blessed Virgin," he said, "because it is mamma's birthday."

Jim flushed. "So it is, Phil," he cried.

"Why didn't you remind me of it before? What a queer chap you are!"

Carola saw how deeply disappointed Phil was, and cast about in her mind for a way to console him, like the kind child she was. "I'll tell you, Phil," she whispered. "Don't feel bad that the cross faded; the Blessed Virgin knows you made it for her."

"And Jim," Phil interrupted.

"I mean you and Jim," Carola went on. "This afternoon I'll bring my statue of the Blessed Virgin over to the island, and we'll make a shrine for her all maidenhair and flowers."

"Will Carl laugh?" whispered Phil.

"No, of course not," Carola said, a little hurt by this doubt of her adored brother. "Carl is much better than any one," she added with conviction. "We'll make a lovely shrine, and keep your mamma's birthday as nice as we can."

"I love you, Carola," Phil whispered by

way of thanks, slipping his hand into hers as they went up the church steps.

The sermon was on the love of one's neighbor, and in its course the priest suggested that where a person was very disagreeable to one it was well to try doing kindnesses for that person, which was almost certain to make one like that person better, besides being quite certain to call forth love and gratitude towards the one who did the kindness. Phil listened intently, and that afternoon he and Carola discussed the plan while they sat in a shady dell on Dimanche Island, before the shrine which they had made for Carola's little statue of the Blessed Virgin. The end of the discussion was that they decided that no one could well be more disagreeable than Miss Keturah, so no one could be a better subject on whom to try the experiment.

The result was that they gathered a bunch of elderberry-blossoms for Miss Keturah, and Carola furnished the blue ribbon from the end of her braid to add a touch of elegance by tying the flowers with it. A few ferns made the bouquet complete, and it was so pretty that the children surveyed it with profound satisfaction, and, feeling mollified towards Miss Keturah in preparing such a pleasant surprise for her, hoped that as the first part of the effect of doing a kindness, which had been promised by the sermon, had been fulfilled, the second would also follow.

Phil took the flowers to Miss Keturah at once after they came home from Dimanche Island. "Here, Miss Keturah," he said, his pale face flushed, and his big gray eyes bright with anticipation, "I brought you these flowers, and I hope you'll like them."

"For the land sakes!" snapped Miss Keturah, laying down the "Report of the American Board of Foreign Missions" which she had been reading, and looking at Phil's tribute with extreme disfavor. "What do you think I want of elderberry-blows? They're no good except for tea, and they're as common as dirt. Don't you let them shatter on my floor; you take 'em straight out and throw 'em on the dirt-heap. Here, wait; where'd you get that blue ribbon?"

"Carola let me have it," said Phil faintly.

"Well, you take it off that bunch of flowers. No, give it to me; you'll shatter 'em most likely if you untie 'em. There, I'll take that ribbon and give it to Mis' Blake. I sh'd like to know what right Carola has to give her ribbons away for you to play with. I d' know what her mother's thinking of to let her traipse around with a pair of children from land knows where. There, I'll shake these blows into the coal-hod, and don't you bring home any more trash. Now go, and take off your Sunday clothes, and get the cows home."

Phil turned away in silence, with a swelling heart. There was no use in trying to do kindnesses for Miss Keturah; there was something wrong in the theory that doing kindnesses for people made them love you. "I guess the priest made a mistake, Jim," he said plaintively, as he finished telling his brother of his experience.

Jim ground his teeth angrily. "He meant it would make people who had souls love one another," he said. "Miss Keturah must have got her shoe-sole in her, instead of the real kind. I'm sure her soul's harder than the toughest leather."

CHAPTER VI.

MISS KETURAH'S NIECE.

THERE was the stir and bustle of preparation over Stony Brook Farm. As early as their return from taking the cows to pasture, Jim and Phil found Miss Keturah rinsing out the muslin curtains of the spare bedroom which she had already washed. "I guess I'll keep you 'round the house to-day," she said to Jim. "I'll want you to do a good many little chores, and maybe I'll need things from the village."

This sounded cheerful to the boys, who longed to be together; but they soon found that there would be as little chance to see each other that day as if Jim had been hoeing the corn, and Phil washing dishes. Jim had to nail up the curtains when they were ironed, help take down all the dishes from the china-closet, move the furniture out of every room while Miss Keturah swept, untie the parlor furniture from its brown holland covers, and do many other things, besides going down to the village three times for forgotten articles, from tacks to lemons.

The day was very sultry, and Phil, who had been kept equally busy, began to droop, and even strong Jim was thoroughly tired; but Miss Keturah's strength was unflagging, and she seemed no more weary when she ceased her labors at half-past three in the afternoon than she had been at half-past six in the morning, when they had first seen her.

"There," said Miss Keturah, drawing a long breath of satisfaction as she looked around the thoroughly renovated house, " now I'm goin' to the deepo, and you can be ready to take the horse out when I come back."

"Expect company, Miss Flint?" asked

Jim; he had not ventured before to inquire the cause of these tremendous preparations.

"Yes; my niece's coming to stay here the rest of the summer," Miss Keturah replied. "She's my sister's child; she married a kind of cousin of ours who's a big mill-owner, and this girl's used to about the best there is. I don't want she should find things in a mess, even if she is a little girl."

"A little girl!" cried Jim, much surprised.

"Well, she's about your age," Miss Keturah said. "I ain't goin' to have her tell her mother, when she goes home, I ain't a clean housekeeper. I don't put on so much style as her folks, but Ellen Frances, her mother, never would have kep' things the way I do if she'd had to do her own work, I know that much. Now you get along, and mind your own affairs," added Miss Keturah sharply, suddenly realizing that she was talking at some length to her farm-boy.

"Now I wonder, Jim, if she could be anything like Carola," said Phil, as they watched Miss Keturah drive away.

" 'Tisn't likely, if she's Miss Flint's kin," said Jim contemptuously.

In due time the buggy came creaking back up the road, and Jim, and Phil half-hiding behind him, caught a glimpse of a little figure, surmounted by a hat with many nodding plumes, sitting up very straight beside Miss Keturah. As the carriage turned into the yard, the boys saw that a mass of very light hair hung below the feathers, and a pair of light-blue eyes looked out from under the hat-brim. Seeing Jim, the girl asked: "Who's the boy, Aunt Ket?" And Jim heard the reply: "A poor boy that I took in to help around for his board," and his cheeks were very red when he came forward to take the horse's head.

They did not see the new arrival again until after supper; then she came out to the barn, and surveyed Jim and Phil with a critical stare that caused Rags to show his teeth, and retreat growling beneath the hay-wagon.

"Do you like staying here?" the young lady demanded, having finished her survey.

Jim hesitated. "I think it's a pretty place," he said at last.

"Oh! don't mind me," the girl said. "I don't care about Stony Brook Farm. Isn't it horrid to work for your board?"

Jim flushed. "I don't know as it's horrid to work for your living," he said.

"How do you get on with Aunt Ket? Isn't she a terror?" that lady's niece inquired next.

Jim looked at her wonderingly; it seemed to him that it would be as well if she spoke less disrespectfully of her aunt, though he could not help agreeing with her opinion. "Oh! don't pretend you like her, for she's simply hateful," the girl went on. "Say, what's your name? Mine's Ella May Flint—don't you think Ella May's a nice name?"

"My name is Jim Upper, and my brother's Phil Upper," said Jim, discreetly avoiding expressing an opinion as to her name.

"Upper—what a name! Ought to be Lower anyhow," said Ella May, laughing. "What do you do for fun here? Do you know anybody—got any friends?"

"Only the Blakes," said Jim.

"The Blakes! Yes, I guess so," cried Ella May derisively. "What are you giving us? Do you s'pose I believe that yarn? Why, even I don't play with the Blakes; they think I'm not good enough for them, they're so stuck up."

"You needn't believe it if you don't want to," said Jim. "It's true all the same, and they're not one bit stuck up. Carl says his mother only wants him to go with good boys, but she don't mind if they're poor ones."

"Well, I'll believe you go with the Blake twins when I see it," said Ella May, turning on her heel.

Questions put to her aunt brought out the astounding fact that Jim had spoken the truth, and Ella May treated him with something like respect when she found that the children of the richest people in the village did not scorn him. Jim found her favor rather a burden; he disliked everything about her, from her vain and vulgar manners to her habit of tormenting every animal on the place if it came in her way. As to Phil, he shrank from her with unspeakable dread, and Rags barked at her frantically whenever she appeared.

The favor that Ella May condescended to show the boys was of short duration, however. On the fourth day after her arrival she came into the barn early in the afternoon with a pleasant manner that Jim had already learned presaged mischief. He was occupied cutting his initials, and Dandy's—"the colt," as the lively two-year-old chestnut was called—on the side of the latter's stall. Dandy was as full of mischief as he was handsome, and that is saying much. No one was allowed to put him in harness, but Jim took him for exercise daily, and there had come to be a cordial friendship between the horse boy and the human boy, born of their youth and understanding of one another.

Ella May stood in silence by Jim's elbow a moment, watching the flourish he added to the last stroke of the D, which followed the J and U already carved.

"Funny you happen to be doing that," she remarked in what Jim called her "will-you-walk-into-my-parlor-said-the-spider-to-the-fly tones," "because I wanted to ask you something about Dandy. Did you know Aunt Ket's gone off for the whole afternoon, and maybe to supper?"

"Yes; I harnessed Jenny for her to go," said Jim.

"That's so; of course you did," said Ella

May cordially. "Well, I want you should harness Dandy for me in the buggy, for I'm going to drive him."

"Well, I guess not," said Jim promptly and decidedly.

"Oh! now, don't be nasty and disobliging," said Ella May, not losing her honeyed tones, though her eyes flashed. "Please, and I'll do you a favor any time you need one."

"I don't want any favors," said Jim gruffly. "I'll do what's right, and I only want what's right. I wouldn't harness Dandy for you, not if you were to get on your knees to beg me. First of all, he'd kill you, and most likely himself. And next, Miss Flint trusted me to take care of things, and I'm going to do what she wants done whether she's here to see or isn't. So I won't harness Dandy, and that's flat."

"You will harness him, because I tell you to," screamed Ella May, flying into a sudden passion and stamping her foot. "You're nothing but a beggar-boy, and don't you dare disobey. You harness that horse, I tell you."

Jim looked at her, and began to whistle. "Well, where's my fine lady now?" he asked. "Don't you get excited, Miss Ella May Flint, and don't call names either, for it's not pretty and doesn't do any good. I'll obey your aunt, but you can't make me mind you and do what I've no business to. Come on, Rags!" and whistling his little friend to follow, Jim strolled out of the stable.

"You'll be sorry for this, Jim Upper, see if you're not," shrieked Ella May at his retreating back.

"I'm awful sorry for you already," retorted Jim over his shoulder. "Better cool off; it's too hot to be so mad."

Left to herself, Ella May wasted a few moments in tears of helpless anger; then she dried them, and set about beginning the sorrow she had prophesied for Jim. She was a reckless child, without fear, and accustomed to her own way in everything. First she slipped Dandy's halter, and led him out. Although she did not know how to harness, she had often watched the operation, and felt sure that she could perform it; so she next got the collar over Dandy's head, and adjusted all the buckles and straps as she thought they should be. The young horse stood so patiently during this process that she felt sure that his liveliness had been much exaggerated; he even allowed her to back him into the shafts, and she was so elated by this final triumph that she entirely failed to notice that she had merely slipped the traces over the whiffletree, and had forgotten to fasten them. She sprang into the buggy, seized the reins, and slapped them on Dandy's back, crying: "Get up!" at the top of her shrill voice, looking around to see if Jim were watching, and prepared with the whip to give him a sharp cut if he should attempt to stop her.

Dandy started; he had been in harness several times before, but only in a light sulky to break him, and the rattle of the buggy behind him aroused every nerve in his body. Jim, standing by the well-curb, saw a gleam of a triumphant face, a dash of something whirling by him, and realized that the wilful girl had carried out her plan, and Dandy was running away. To be perfectly truthful, it must be confessed that Jim's anxiety was for the safety of his beloved Dandy, and not for Ella May; but he could do nothing to save either, for, almost before he could take in what had happened, they were out of sight down the road.

At first Ella May could hardly contain her delight, and she even flourished her whip, snapping it out at one side of the buggy, adding to Dandy's frenzied speed and her own sense of triumph.

But as she sped on down the village street, and found that she owed her safety to the good behavior of the farmers' horses which she passed, for she could not guide Dandy, and as people came out to gaze at her, and she caught their groans of pity as she flashed by, she realized that the colt was running away, and all her courage left her, and deadly fear paralyzed every muscle. It was this alone, that she was unable to move, that kept her from jumping from the carriage and being dashed to pieces.

Straight through the village Dandy ran, past the post-office, where the loungers threw up their hands and prophesied death to the child alone in the carriage. Down a hill beyond the village boundary they tore in safety, though at the top Ella May, looking down, felt sure the end had come. She owed her preservation at last to her own bad harnessing, for, going up another hill, the traces slipped from their place, Dandy sprang forward free, and was quickly lost to sight over the hill-top, while the buggy rattled backward down the hill alone, turned to one side at the foot, and upset Ella May into the blackberry-vines beside the road, none the worse for her escapade, except for a few bruises and scratches and a thorough fright.

It was a long walk home, and the trembling girl had plenty of time to reflect on her aunt's wrath, the possible loss of Dandy, and to determine to lie out of the scrape if she could.

"Now what's this I've heard in the village, as I came home, about your taking the colt, and his being lost?" demanded Miss Keturah, entering the kitchen, where Phil and Jim were at supper, and Ella May seated in the window, too miserable to eat.

"Aunt Keturah, it's not my fault; you won't blame me when you hear about it," said Ella May, rising to meet her aunt with an assumption of frankness. "He," she continued, pointing at Jim, "harnessed Dandy; and when I begged him not to, he said you were away, and he'd do what he'd a mind to. So he was just getting in the buggy, and I jumped in the other side and pushed him back, and he tumbled off the step, and then Dandy ran away with me in the buggy, and it wasn't my fault."

Jim listened to this story with cheeks getting redder and redder. When Ella May ceased speaking, he sprang to his feet, exclaiming: "Miss Keturah——" But Miss Keturah cut him short with a gesture. "You go on and tend to your chores; I don't want to hear a word," she said.

"But only let me tell you," Jim implored.

"I won't listen; do as I tell you," Miss Keturah commanded, and Jim had to obey.

As soon as the door had shut on him and Phil, Miss Keturah turned on Ella May. "Now, Ella May Flint," she said sternly, "you've done about enough for one day, and I don't want you should lie to me. I know there ain't one word of truth in what you've just told me. You needn't try to make me believe that boy would do anything to hurt that colt, because I know just what store he sets by him; besides, though I can't say I care much about those two children, I can trust 'em both, and that's more'n I could ever say of you, if you are my sister's child. So you go straight up to your room and go to bed, and when I've had my supper I'm coming up to give you a whipping you'll remember."

"Aunt Keturah, you won't dare lay your hand on me," said Ella May, flushing with anger. "Even my own father and mother never whip me."

"H'm! so I should s'pose," said Miss Keturah dryly. "And as to daring to whip you, Ella May Flint, don't talk about daring, because if a niece of mine took a valuable horse, and maybe lost it for me, and then tried to lie out of it by putting the blame on an innocent person, I'd whip her if she was twenty, let alone twelve. So you go up-stairs and wait for me." And Ella May went up and waited; nor did she wait in vain.

CHAPTER VII.

PHIL'S TREASURES.

A WEEK after Ella May's adventure, Dandy was returned from a town ten miles distant, in response to an advertisement of his loss posted by the sheriff on all the available spots within his district. He came back lame in one leg, and his recovery cost Miss Keturah ten dollars, neither of which facts made her more inclined to excuse her niece's naughtiness.

Jim saw that Miss Keturah had no doubt as to who was the culprit, and made no further attempt to tell the story of that afternoon. Indeed, it was the first consolation that he had received in his hard service of Miss Keturah to find that she trusted him without this explanation, and he felt a glow of pride that made him almost like that stern maiden. But between him and Ella May there was henceforth war. Ella May could not forgive him for having done right when she wanted him to do wrong, nor for her failure to make her aunt believe that he was untrustworthy. She lost no chance of doing all kinds of mean and spiteful things to him, but Jim was so hard at work all the day long that these chances were fewer than she would have liked, and besides he paid so little attention to what she did that some of her best-laid plans for making him uncomfortable failed entirely. So she turned her talents towards tormenting poor little Phil, who shared her dislike; and here she succeeded better, not only because the little fellow was more about the house, but because he was so sensitive and easily hurt.

In the darkest corner of the barn chamber which the boys occupied stood a wooden box bearing on each end a bright red label setting forth the superiority of the starch it formerly held. Now the box contained Phil's chief earthly treasures, treasures that would not have been negotiable in any market of the world, unless there be somewhere, not set down on any map, a country called Kindergarten-land. Phil had picked up these precious things in his wanderings, had preserved them carefully through all dangers, and now that he and Jim had something like a room of their own, albeit rough and dreary, he had procured a box for his possessions, and when he had a chance stole off to gloat over them. None but a child could have said what form and beauty this queer collection bore in Phil's eyes. To another they looked like the gilded stopper of a cologne-bottle, a few stained advertisement-cards, half a dozen odd-shaped stones, a bit of chain, and a doll with one foot missing and a sad crack in her battered cheek, which, boy though he was and eight years old, was Phil's chief possession. Sometimes he ventured to take them from the box, and steal away with them out of doors, and spread them in all their beauty in the soft grass. On these occasions he added to them blossoms from the fields, and, the silvery silk of the ripening corn, and wreathed his treasures round with these added beauties, fancying no one knew what pretty things of the maimed objects which his childish fairy-touch could turn precious.

One day Miss Keturah had gone to North Branscome, and Ella May appeared nowhere about. Phil, grown bold in the utter silence of the kitchen, brought all his treasures down, and spread them out on the broad upper step of the back door. The advertisement-cards he framed in tiny blossoms, the stones he laid on some bright-colored scraps of woollen which he had picked up, and the doll he laid on a corn-silk couch, with corn-silk covering all but her face like a drapery. As he arranged and rearranged these things he crooned a happy little song, interrupted occasionally by short conversations between him and the invalid doll, whom he had named Carola. He did not see Ella May come down the back stairs, nor did he know that she was near him until her shadow fell on the step as she crept to the door to see what he was doing. He looked up with a sudden start, and Ella May laughed. "My! won't you catch it when Aunt Ket comes, littering up the place with that trash!" she remarked.

Phil hastily started to gather up his treasures, but had only clutched the cologne-stopper, when Ella May was too quick for him. Holding him off with one of her strong hands, with the other she swept every poor little scrap of his possessions into her apron, and then darted with them into the kitchen, purposely scattering the flowers and corn-silk all over the clean floor which was her aunt's pride. "Oh, please give me them; oh, please, *please* don't!" cried poor Phil in anguish, running after her and clutching her skirts imploringly. "Oh! give me them; I've had them so long;

don't hurt them. Oh, Ella May! oh, Ella May!"

"Hurt them! Well, I'd like to know how you could hurt that stuff," said Ella May, turning them over roughly in her apron. "No wonder they say you're half-witted."

Phil burst out crying. "If only you'll let me have them, I'll put them all away," he implored. "I didn't litter up the floor; oh! I didn't do any harm at all with them."

And at this moment Miss Keturah entered. "See, Aunt Ket," cried Ella May, turning to meet her. "See how this boy has been cluttering up the house because you were away."

"Oh! I didn't; I just played on the back step," began Phil.

But Miss Keturah cut him short. "Get the broom and sweep it up this minute," she said without waiting to hear more.

"I took all this trash away from him," said Ella May, opening her apron to display the pitiful little treasures. "I thought he hadn't ought to make a muss just 'cause you weren't here to stop him."

Miss Keturah was very warm, and besides was thoroughly annoyed. She had driven over to North Branscome to collect money due her, and had failed, and more than anything else in the world Miss Keturah cared for her money. She was not in a mood to be just, much less patient, and, after giving a hasty glance at the contents of the apron, she said sharply: "Throw them into the fire."

Ella May needed no second bidding. The lid of the stove was off, and she quickly crammed everything she had seized into it, first taking the precaution to open the drafts.

For a moment Phil stood petrified by horror, and then the tin pans on the wall seemed to dance to the reverberations of his cry. "Oh, Carola! oh, my beautiful, beautiful darling! Oh, you wicked, dreadful woman! Oh, save them, save them!" In a frenzy of grief poor Phil ran to the stove to rescue the companions of his past wanderings and present loneliness. Ella May caught his arms to stay him, but the usually gentle child pushed her from him so violently that she fell on the painted floor, and Miss Keturah darted forward to avenge her.

"Here, young man, what's come over you? I guess I'll have to show you who's mistress here," she remarked, holding him at arm's length, struggling impotently in her powerful grasp.

"Let me go!" screamed the frantic child, "They're burning this very minute. Oh, you cruel, wicked, awful woman! They're mine, mine; you haven't any right to touch them."

"Look here," said Miss Keturah coolly but grimly, surveying his dilated eyes and crimson cheeks and helpless struggles. "I ain't going to let you sauce me, and it's far from pretty to call names; I'm goin' to whip you."

But Phil's feeble strength had burned out; he did not hear the threat. Realizing with sudden keenness that he had been bereft, that nothing could give him back what he had lost, his poor little head fell forward, and he slipped through Miss Keturah's hands in a dead faint on the floor.

"Well, I want to know!" exclaimed Miss Keturah, bending down to make sure that she was right. "If he ain't fainted! Ella May, throw some water over him. I'd like to know what under the sun made him act up like this."

To do Miss Keturah justice, she had not the smallest notion of the tragedy enacted; nothing could have made her understand how dear to Phil were the worthless things which she had destroyed. If she had known, she would hardly have consigned them to the flames; but since to her they were fragments of no value, Phil's grief was to her but "a tantrum," to be dealt with accordingly.

After a few moments the little boy opened his eyes again, and presently sat up. Looking about him wonderingly, his glance fell upon the stove, and as this recalled his loss to him, he fell back upon the floor and, burying his head in his arm, sobbed quietly.

"You said you'd whip him, Aunt Ket," Ella May reminded her. She had watched the scene entirely unmoved, and was not unwilling that Jim's brother should feel the power of her aunt's strong right arm, as she had so recently felt it.

Miss Keturah looked at her niece with some contempt. "I'll wait till he's through fainting," she remarked. "Are you sorry you spoke up so saucy to me?" she asked Phil.

"I—wasn't—saucy," sobbed poor Phil. "I hadn't done—any—harm. I wasn't—in—the—kitchen; she brought—my things—in. I—was—out—on—the—back—step. I didn't —litter, and I'd had those—things—so long— and I — loved — them—oh, I — did—love— them!" and Phil's feeble voice was lost in sobs.

"Ella May Flint, didn't you tell me he was

cluttering up the kitchen?" demanded Miss Keturah.

"Yes, ma'am," said Ella May boldly, "and I thought he hadn't ought to."

Phil shook his head sadly in his arm. "I don't care now," he said, "because they're all gone; but I'm telling you the truth, because Jim and I hate lying."

Miss Keturah turned on Ella May sharply. "I guess you've no need wait here," she said. "If you've got anything to do, I won't hinder you doing it. And you, Phil, can lay on the sofa over there, if you want to, and keep quiet a spell, for most likely your fainting's left you feeling streakéd."

"No, thank you, ma'am," said Phil, rising slowly. "I guess I'll go out of doors somewhere. I'll see if I can find Rags."

Miss Keturah watched the little figure dragging wearily down the path under the big lilacs, and her heart misgave her. "Well, he beats me," she said aloud. "I never saw anything like him. Mebbe I'd better not have burned his truck, but mercy on us! none but a child that wasn't quite right would set store by such things."

That night Phil ate no supper, and his cheeks were crimson. Miss Keturah eyed him uneasily as he emptied his goblet of water for the fourth time. "I sh'd think you'd better eat something, and not do nothing but drink water," she said. "I'll give you some preserves if you can't eat plain bread."

Phil shook his head languidly, while Jim stared, wondering if Miss Keturah were going to die.

"I'm sleepy," said Phil. "I don't want my supper; I'd like to go right to bed, if you'll excuse me, please."

"Sick, Tiddy boy?" asked Jim anxiously, forgetting that he had an audience as he used the name his mother had called his little brother, borrowed from Phil's baby lips before he could speak his own name plainly.

"No, Jim; sleepy," said Phil, trying not to cry, as he pushed his chair back and got down.

As soon as his evening tasks were done, Jim hastened to the barn chamber. He found Phil asleep, a high fever burning his slender frame, and his cheeks bright against the unbleached pillow-case. Tight clasped in one little hot hand was the stopper of the cologne-bottle, the only thing saved from the wreck of his treasures. As the light of Jim's candle fell on his closed eyes he began to mutter. Attracted by the first words, Jim listened, and thus gathered the story of the afternoon's suffering.

Jim's own cheeks grew red as he caught it. "The old grindstone!" he muttered between his set teeth. "How could she be so hard on Phil? Poor little chap! I wish I was a man, and could take care of him right." He made haste to undress and get the light out, then rung out a towel in the cool spring-water with which he had filled a broken pitcher generously accorded them by Miss Keturah. With this he bathed the burning little hands and wet the hot head and tangled curly hair. Then he turned the bed so that the soft west wind could come in through the open window and cool the fevered child.

The last glow of a glorious sunset still lingered faintly in the west as Jim knelt down by the window to say his prayers. "O God, give Phil a good time, and never mind me," he whispered. Rags came up softly, and licked Jim's clasped hands, and he crept in beside Phil, who had grown quiet, comforted by that mute caress, feeling that when a little dog could be so faithful God would surely take care of Phil.

CHAPTER VIII.

GOOD FOR EVIL.

FORTUNATELY for Phil, there were but two days between his bereavement and Sunday, a day that largely made up to him for the troubles of the week. Carl and Carola had a message to carry for their mother near Stony Brook Farm, so they stopped for Jim and Phil to go to Dimanche Island contrary to their usual custom, which was to meet halfway.

On the previous Sunday Ella May had watched with envious eyes the boys setting forth, as she stood swinging the tassel of the sitting-room window-shade, dreading the dreariness which Miss Keturah seemed to consider a necessary part of keeping holy the Sabbath-day. In vain had she plied Jim and Phil all day Monday with questions as to where they and the twins had spent Sunday afternoon; the only thing that she was able to discover was that they had a secret, and this did not lessen her desire to find out what was really done. Now, when Carl and Carola stood waiting under the lilac-bushes for Jim and Phil, Ella May came forth and joined them.

"Ain't you coming in?" she asked. "It's cooler inside."

"No, thank you," said Carl, "we don't mind being a little warm."

"That's an awful nice dress you've got on," remarked Ella May sweetly to Carola. "Come from New York?"

"Yes," said Carola; "I'm glad you like it."

"I'd just love to see New York; it must be an awful big place," continued Ella May.

"It is pretty big," assented Carl.

"I've been to Lawrence, Massachusetts,

Did you ever go there?" asked Ella May.

"No, never," said Carola.

"Oh, my! that's a big place, too," cried Ella May with forced enthusiasm. "That's where they make cotton and calicoes; my pa took me to the mills. My! it's grand there! It's big, too, maybe it's 'most as big as New York. You just ought to see Lawrence."

"I should like to," murmured Carola politely, as she shifted from one foot to the other, and wished the boys would make haste.

"Do you like playing with poor boys?" inquired Ella May next. "I don't think my ma would allow me to play with everybody."

"There wouldn't be room for everybody, even if she would," Carl said quickly. "You don't suppose we've got room for everybody on the island?"

Carola poked him warningly. Ella May's sharp ears and eyes noted the slip and the poke; she had found out one thing—they went to an island. But all that she said was: "My! ain't you funny! It's dreadful lonesome and poky here Sunday afternoons," she added plaintively. "The boys go off, and Aunt Ket's so cross."

"But you don't play with the boys anyway; you just said so," said Carl.

Ella May bit her lip. Carola was such a gentle little soul that she felt sorry for the discomfiture even of Ella May; she did not know the history of the past week, of the destruction of Phil's treasures, or perhaps even her heart would have been steeled against its cause; but as it was she tried to turn aside the severity of her brother's retort.

"You have a pretty hat, and how nice your daisies are!" she said.

Ella May tossed her head sullenly, with a vicious glance at Carola's own simple sailor. "I wouldn't wear one without flowers," she said, and then remembered that it would not do to be rude to the Blakes if she wanted to be asked to go with them. "You'd go pretty near crazy if you was me, all alone here," she said.

Just then Jim and Phil and Rags came around the corner, to the great relief of the twins.

"Let's meet them, Carol," said Carl. "Good-by."

"Oh! wait a minute," implored Ella May, growing desperate as she saw her chances lessening. "Won't you come just to see me some day? I'd love to have you."

"Thank you," said Carola, too honest to say that she would. "You're very kind. And I'd ask you to go with us, but I really can't, because we haven't any right to show our place to any one, for it's a secret, and besides we do something now on Sunday afternoons that we couldn't have any one else there when we do. Good-by."

Baffled and angry, Ella May watched them depart, Carl and Jim, Carola and Phil. The new employment of Sunday afternoon to which Carola had alluded was the teaching of catechism. Every Sunday Mrs. Blake gave her children a little lesson in the catechism, and every Sunday afternoon Carola handed the lesson on to Phil.

It seemed to Phil that he had never had such a happy afternoon on Dimanche Island as this one. He told the story of his loss to Carola, and she comforted him; and after he had cried a little he felt better than he had thought he could ever feel again, and forgot all about himself in listening to the story of the boy martyr Tarcisius, which Carola read him from "Fabiola."

While the children were thus spending a peaceful Sunday afternoon under the whispering trees, Ella May, with her soul full of envy and jealousy, was planning to discover their secret, and revenge herself for its being theirs to the exclusion of her.

Monday afternoon, when Phil had finished

wiping Miss Keturah's dishes and had gone to sit under the big maple which shaded the side of the back yard, Ella May followed him, and stood looking at him for a moment without speaking. Finally she said, speaking suddenly, and with her sharp eyes fixed on Phil's face to note the effect: "I'm going to the island."

Phil started. "What island?" he cried.

"The island where you and the Blakes go on Sundays," Ella May replied. "I dare you to say you haven't got an island."

Phil was silent.

"I'm going," Ella May said, turning on her heel; "and when I get there you'll be sorry you weren't decent, and asked me to join you."

Phil sprang up to follow her. Ella May stalked on, wondering how she should find the island, but not betraying her uncertainty. Phil walked after her, afflicted at her going, and trying in vain to think of a way to hinder her. Rags, who had been with Jim at work in the field, was coming home at this moment, tired of the heat, and feeling that there was no use in following Jim in the broiling sun when Phil was at home and would be glad to see him. Meeting his smaller master at this opportune moment, he gave several barks of welcome, and joined him at once.

Ella May went straight to the river's edge, knowing, of course, that the island must be somewhere in the stream. She walked up the river-bank, puzzled how to attain her object, and at last she halted. "You'd better tell me where your old island is," she said. "Maybe if you do I won't hurt it."

Phil thought of the games and books hidden in the hollow tree which they had made their cupboard, and his heart misgave him as to their probable fate if Ella May should discover them. Still he could not betray a secret. "I can't tell you, Ella May," he said. "It's our secret, and we've promised solemn true, black and blue, not to tell any one about it. Won't you please be nice, and not look for it? We wouldn't any of us bother you."

Ella May sniffed contemptuously. "I s'pose you think you behave nice to me when you go off before my very eyes, and never ask me to come along," she retorted.

"Well, but——" began Phil, and stopped. He had a confused desire to explain the right of every one to choose his or her own friends, but did not know how to put his thoughts into words.

"Yes, 'but,'" repeated Ella May. "'But' I'll find your island, and you'll be sorry." Just how she would have succeeded in doing this is not clear, for the approach to the island was concealed by trees, but Rags innocently helped her. When they were opposite the island, the small dog, taking it for granted that Phil was bound there as he had been the day before, and all the other times when he had come to this point, plunged into the water, and soon stood on the shore of the island, barking joyously. Ella May quickly espied the end of the plank which was their draw-bridge. Laughing triumphantly she ran across, and Phil followed, fearing what she was about to do. It hurt him dreadfully to see Ella May standing in their beloved little nook, but it was worse when, catching sight of the piece of old carpet which they had drawn over the opening of the hollow tree to keep its contents dry, she pulled it aside and had all that was in it out in a moment.

"I'm going to throw all these things into the river," she said, holding "Fabiola" and a game in each hand.

"Indeed you mustn't; they're Carola's and Carl's, and it's stealing to take other people's things," cried Phil. But there was never any use in trying to stop Ella May doing anything that she wanted to do, especially if it was mischief. Running to the river's edge, on the opposite side of the island from the one on which they had crossed, Ella May threw the game into the water, and then flung "Fabiola" after it with all her might. But in this last throw something happened. Her foot slipped, she lost her balance, and fell into the water which had just swallowed up the game and book. Shallow as the river was, Ella May began to sink, and Phil remembered that Carl had said that a treacherous bog formed the bed of the stream on that side.

Ella May, realizing that she was held fast, filled the air with screams, and prayers to Phil to help her. Phil was only eight, and very small of his age, while Ella May was a big girl of twelve; but little Phil had the soul of a hero in his frail body, and he made ready to try to save Ella May. First he threw out a dead sapling to her, but he could not hold his end, so that attempt was useless. Then gravely stripping off his little jacket, he plunged in after her, and tried to draw her out. Encouraged by the touch of even such feeble little hands as Phil's, Ella May tried more collectedly to help herself, and, at last, after the greatest exertions on the part of Phil, he actually did manage to get Ella May up where she could seize some of the rushes by the bank, and, as he pushed, she pulling, dragged herself upon the island and was safe. But there was no one to help Phil out, and he had sunk down to his waist in the miry mud, and was held fast.

Rags had been running up and down the bank like a dog gone distracted, all the time that Phil was trying to rescue Ella May, and now, seeing his little master's plight, he set out across the tiny island to the shore, and disappeared over the hill, barking furiously.

Ella May stood on the island, crying and wringing her hands as she looked helplessly at Phil in the mire from which he had rescued her.

Phil himself reminded her of her duty. "You'd better go call some one," he said.

"I can't get out, but I guess I'm not going to sink any more; I don't feel any lower than I did. Only please hurry, Ella May."

"Seem's as if 'twas mean to leave you," said Ella May, turning slowly.

"I'm all right," said brave little Phil, "only do please hurry."

Every moment seemed an hour to the poor child left alone a prisoner in the mire; but he tried to say his prayers, and after that he even tried to whistle a little to keep his courage up. The worst of it all was the deadly chill creeping through his frame. The day was very warm, his walk had heated him, and the great effort he had made to help Ella May had sent the perspiration from every pore, and now, standing in the shade in the cold bog, it seemed to Phil that a chill was entering his very heart, and his teeth chattered, and his hands began to grow blue as he waited. The longest hour must have an end at last, and Phil's trial was over before quite an hour had gone by. But it was Rags who proved the speedier messenger. The little dog had met Phil's friend, Seth Peters, the herb-gatherer, and being used to Rags, and familiar with the manner of speech of dumb things generally, Seth had quickly understood that something was wrong when Rags tried to tell him so. Running at full speed, he followed the dog to the scene of the accident, and his long, strong arm quickly rescued poor Phil from his plight, and laid him on the dry land.

But when this was done, Seth saw that the work was by no means accomplished, and that Phil was in greater danger from cold than he had been from drowning. He wore no coat in which he could wrap the child, so, taking him in his arms, he ran over the fields to Stony Brook Farm, trying to chafe his hands and limbs as he ran.

"Give me hot water and blankets, Miss Keturah, quick!" he cried, bursting into Miss Keturah's kitchen. "Get your kettle on, and fix ginger tea; there ain't a minute to lose."

Miss Keturah did as she was directed, and she and Seth worked hard for an hour to restore Phil to something like warmth. At last they laid him in warm blankets before the kitchen fire, and for the first time paused to think.

"I wonder how it happened?" said Miss Keturah.

Seth shook his head. "I'll come around again later," he said, once more conscious of himself and his shyness.

"It happened because I tumbled in the mire doing something bad, and Phil saved me," said a voice behind them. They turned, and saw Ella May, who had heard her aunt's question, standing tear-stained, mud-stained, and ashamed in the doorway.

CHAPTER IX.

PHIL GETS ACQUAINTED.

PHIL was ill, but not, he thought, very ill; only enough so to make all things different, pleasantly different. He had been very dangerously ill for two or three weeks after his exposure to the chill of the water on that hot day in mid-July. The time between then and now seemed to him a confused time of burning fever, sharp pain, struggling for breath, and queer sights and sounds that made waking and sleeping indistinguishable from one another.

But that time was past, and now he was quite well again, or rather he ought to be, for he was up, and about the house, and there seemed to be nothing the matter with him except a cough; and yet he did not feel like doing anything but sit in the window and watch the trees wave, and turn over listlessly the pages of the many pretty books with which he was now provided. The most perplexing thing to Phil was the change which had come over his little world since that afternoon when he had rescued Ella May. At first he constantly expected that Miss Keturah would order him up from the big rocking-chair in the kitchen, for Miss Keturah abhorred idleness. But, so far from doing this, she frequently warned him not to get tired, and even made special dainty dishes to coax him to eat, which she sometimes succeeded in doing, for Miss Keturah was a famous cook. Nay, more: she went so far as to drive all the way over to North Branscome to buy him a doll, which she brought him with some expression of hope that it would take the place of the one burned in the kitchen stove. The doll was far too highly colored, and perfect in every limb, to take the place of the lost Carola, whose attraction lay, not in the fact of her being a doll, but in some mysterious charm which she wore to Phil's eyes alone; but Phil was much too polite to betray his lack of interest in the newcomer, and would hold and handle the doll in puzzled wonder as to what could have come over Miss Keturah.

Ella May, too, was not the same girl. Her manner to Phil was gentle, and even humble; she waited on him, and tried to think of something to do that would give him pleasure. She offered to read to him, and Phil let her, because she seemed to want to, though she did not read well, and he could hardly recognize some of his favorite passages in the new emphasis she gave them. And one day, to be puzzled over in silence, since he could not tell any one what happened then, Ella

May, sitting by him alone, laid her book on her knee, and tearfully asked Phil if he thought that he could ever forgive her, and begged him to please try to do so. Of course Phil promptly assured her that he did not know what she meant, because he had nothing to forgive, but, on the contrary, thought that she was so kind to him now that he did not know how he should ever be able to repay her when he was quite well; and he meant what he said, and was very sorry that saying it had made Ella May cry quite bitterly.

Then there was Seth Peters, who never came to people's houses, or talked to any one, and yet he came every day to see Phil, and would entertain him by the hour in Miss Keturah's kitchen, though he was sure that Seth dreaded to have people around him almost as much as a wild hare would. It was Seth that kept away the only regret that Phil might have felt in these peaceful days, for, since he could not wander in the fields, Seth brought the fields to him, and supplied him with wild flowers, and all sorts of wonders which only his loving eyes could espy.

Jim, Carl, and Carola could not possibly have been better, Phil would have said before he was ill, and yet even they managed to increase their perfections, and make Phil happier than they had made him heretofore. Not a day passed without the twins appearing at Stony Brook Farm, and always with new plans for entertaining him, and Carola growing sweeter every day, the admiring little invalid thought.

Mrs. Blake came, too, and seemed to have grown so fond of the gentle little boy, that when she took him up in her arms, and rocked him, as she often did, Phil thought that with his eyes shut he could not tell whether his own mamma had come back to take care of him, or he had gone to her in heaven. Dear Jim hovered over Phil more than ever, and Phil sometimes closed all books, and gave himself up to wondering if ever before any little boy had been so kindly treated.

"Not a mite of trouble, just as patient as he can be," he heard Miss Keturah whisper to a neighbor who had come to the door one day to borrow some molasses. "Even if he was a bother, I'd feel 's if I had to take it, because he took sick for Ella May's sake."

"There ain't any chance, is there?" asked the neighbor.

"No, not the least mite," said Miss Keturah decidedly. "Rapid, too, I guess. Never was rugged."

Phil puzzled over what this might mean, and finally gave it up, deciding that they might be speaking of his pulse, which he had heard the doctor say was too rapid.

Under all this kindness Phil came out wonderfully; and those who were doing all in their power to make the little fellow's days happy were rewarded by being allowed to share his pretty fancies and receive his confidence. He was silent Phil no longer, but would talk by the hour, seeming to have laid aside all fear and shyness, expanding like a flower in the pleasant warmth. "I want to tell you," he said one night to Miss Keturah, who had finished her dishes early and had been watching the sunset with him. "I want to tell you, Miss Keturah, that I think it does a person good to be ill."

"Do you?" responded that lady.

"Yes, if they're only a little ill, like me. If I hadn't been ill, do you know I'm afraid I might have gone away from here and never known you at all nor Ella May? I used to think you were a little—not much, but a little—down on me, and didn't care to be good to me, and now you are so nice to me that I feel real ashamed when I think of what I used to think."

"I'm not so sure you need to," said Miss Keturah, and Phil really thought she blushed, or was it the west reflected on her face? "I guess I'm a pretty crabbed old apple, Phil. But I want you should know I'm doing my best for you now."

"Oh, dear me! I don't believe anybody ever had such good people to take care of him," cried Phil hastily. "Miss Keturah, why does it make my breath pull so hard when I talk?"

"That's because you've had pneumony; your lungs ain't strong," said Miss Keturah gently.

"I guess I couldn't tramp very far with Jim," said Phil thoughtfully. "I hope I'll be well enough to go around with him when we get through here."

"There's no more tramping to be done by you, Philly," said Miss Keturah. "Don't you ever worry one mite about the next thing you're goin' to do. Jim shall never want a home, and Mrs. Blake told me herself she meant to look after him."

"Now isn't that just lovely!" cried Phil, so energetically that Rags sprang to kiss his hand. and he was seized with such a fit of coughing that after it he was too exhausted to talk, and lay back in the big chair watching the changing colors of the west. "Do you believe heaven is there?" he asked at last.

"Mebbe; I'm afraid I don't know," said Miss Keturah.

"No," said Phil, accepting her limitations quite seriously. "I'll ask Mrs. Blake; she knows about heaven. I'll tell you what I think. I think there's a big, big gate to heaven, all dark on this side, and all bright and full of jewels on the other. And I think every night God sends the angels to open the gate, and let in all the souls who died that day, and then we see all those colors when the gate swings back."

"Mebbe, Phil," said Miss Keturah again, this time a little huskily. "Do you know what I'm goin' to do?" she said more cheerfully. "I'm goin' to ask the Blakes down to tea with you some day soon, next week say. What day would you rather have 'em?"

"I don't know," said Phil. "I should think you'd better choose, because you'd have to get ready for them."

"Well, I don't care after Monday and Tuesday's past," said Miss Keturah. "S'pose we say Thursday? And they're to be your comp'ny, and you'll sit at the head of the table, and we'll have just 's good a time as we can."

"You're so good to me, Miss Keturah," said Phil gratefully. "I love you just heaps and heaps."

Miss Keturah flushed with pleasure, and Phil, catching a softened look that he had never seen on the stern face until of late, threw both arms around Miss Keturah's neck and kissed her.

Poor Miss Keturah had not had much petting in her life, and she responded awkwardly; but under the angular breast, covered by the unattractive dark purple calico which she wore, a warm glow of love and pity responded to the clinging of Phil's little arms.

Thursday came, and brought with it Phil's guests to tea. Ella May had adorned Rags with an immense bow, and he and Neb, between whom there was rather armed neutrality than peace, made a dignified appearance seated one on each side of the hearth.

Phil was in a little flutter of excitement, for, although the Blakes came to see him daily, an invitation to supper changed this coming into an extraordinary occasion.

Miss Keturah had brought forth all her best china, and had herself donned her best stiff black mohair, while Ella May in her figured rose-colored challie was gorgeous to look upon, and made Phil feel festive and overdressed by pinning a scarlet geranium-blossom in his buttonhole.

Jim's duties for that evening were given to some one else, and he was ready to enjoy the festivity, and keep Phil in countenance in the embarrassing task of presiding at the table.

Carl and Carola had discussed the invitation from every possible conjecture, for why Miss Keturah had so completely changed as to give a tea-party for Phil was both marvellous and alarming.

"Even though Phil did get sick to save Ella May, you wouldn't think she would do this," said Carola. "You don't suppose Phil is much sick, do you?"

But Carl scoffed at this suggestion; and when she saw Phil with his cheeks flushed and eyes bright with the excitement of this his first party, Carola felt assured that Carl was right.

After they had eaten all that they possibly could of Miss Keturah's famous biscuit, golden cake, and perfect lemon-puffs, just as they were rising from the table a most wonderful thing happened to end this remarkable day. A very dapper young man came around under the window, and was heard asking if a little boy called Phil Upper lived there.

"It's a long-lost brother, Phil," whispered Carl.

"It's some one come from your grandfather's lawyers to say you are an earl over in England," said Carola, who had read "Little Lord Fauntleroy."

"For pity's sake, Jim, do you know him?" asked Miss Keturah. "I thought you hadn't any folks."

And then, before any one could reply, the young man came in through the side door to explain his errand. "May I speak to Master Phil Upper?" he said with much suavity.

"That is Phil Upper," said Miss Keturah.

"Well, you're not a very big chap to be a hero, but sometimes there is more pluck tucked away in one small body than there is in three big ones," said the stranger. "How did you save the little girl's life? Come, tell me."

"I didn't save her life; I just pulled her out of the river," said Phil wonderingly.

"Much the same thing," laughed the young man. "Tell me all about it."

"She wouldn't have drowned, I guess, unless she had sunk a lot," said Phil.

"Oh! come now; no shyness," cried the visitor. I'll tell you; I'm on *The Cyclone*, that big New York newspaper, and I'm stopping in the village, where I heard about your adventure. I'm going to make a story out of it, and I want a good one, and I'll get your picture, or maybe a view of Stony Brook Farm, or the little girl's picture—yes, that would be better," he added, catching a look of satisfaction pass over Ella May's face. "We'll have your picture, and the little girl's, and maybe she will tell me the story. How did it all come about, my dear?"

"I was throwing something away," began

Ella May, "and I slipped and fell. It's all boggy there, so I sank down, and Phil jumped in and saved me, and he couldn't get out, because he'd gone down in the mud, so he had to stay there 'most an hour, till Rags—the dog—brought Seth Peters to save him, and he got cold and had pneumonia, and he's been sick ever since."

"Where did all this happen?" asked the young man, making notes.

"Oh! on our secret island, where we play," said Jim.

"Splendid! Make a fine human-interest story," cried the young man.

"I'll tell you that story if you'll come outside, young man," said Miss Keturah, and the young man followed her. She told him how the children had come to her early in the summer, homeless and friendless, having found their way from New York; and she told him much else, so that, when she had finished, the visitor came back to bid Phil good-night with a manner much changed and softened, and a look on his face as if he had himself been touched by a feeling of "human interest."

"It will make a capital story," he said, "and I'm going to write it up in my best style. Only you'll have to let me make the river a few feet deeper, because it will sound better, and newspapers object to telling the truth. Good-night; maybe I'll see you again before I leave Branscome."

The children were so excited that they could scarcely speak after he had gone. To think that Phil's sacrifice should be told in the New York paper for people to read and wonder at!

"Well, Phil, you said last night that you thought you were getting acquainted with people," cried Jim, "and I should say you were! Only think how many folks will read that story in *The Cyclone*, and know you although you don't know them."

"It's so queer," cried Phil. "Why, I didn't do anything nice. Don't let him say I did, Jim. Isn't it queer? I'm only little me, and everybody acts as though I were somebody else."

CHAPTER X.

INTO THE SUNSET.

THE still August days slipped by, and September had come. The blackberry-vines hung over the stone walls all bronze and dull red; the fields which Jim had sown in June were yellow with the ripened grain.

Phil was no better; on the contrary, Phil grew weaker every day, and even the children began to realize that silent little Phil was slipping away from them into heaven. Jim went about with a face so full of grief that it was pitiable to see, and with the grief burned fierce resistance to dear little Phil's dying for Ella May.

"It's bad enough to lose him," he said to Mrs. Blake, to whom alone he opened his heart, "but I can't, I can't bear it when I think that if that girl hadn't been so mean about hunting out our secret, and throwing away those things, and Phil hadn't tried to save her after all that, he would have been well, and stayed with me maybe till we were old. She isn't worth dying for, Mrs. Blake, and Phil, the best, sweetest little fellow that ever walked this earth, is just thrown away for that good-for-nothing girl."

"Ah! Jim, Phil is not thrown away," said Mrs. Blake gently. "We are all better and happier for knowing the dear, unselfish little soul. And look at what he has done! Miss Keturah will never be the same woman again, because of loving this child, and being sorry for her hardness and injustice towards him. And Ella May has grown so gentle, so considerate, so humble, that Carola says she would never know her, and she will grow up, perhaps, a true, good woman because of Phil. And I am sure he has done my children any amount of good. Nothing pure and sweet and unselfish is ever lost, dear Jim, and little Phil has not lived, nor will he die, in vain."

"I can't, I can't, I can't give him up," sobbed poor Jim.

"Not even to let him be safe from trouble and sin forever? Not even to be as unselfish as he is, Jim?" suggested Mrs. Blake.

And Jim squared his shoulders manfully, and said: "I'll try."

Mrs. Blake had devoted herself to the sick child, and had even wished to remove him to her big house, where she thought that he might be better cared for, but Miss Keturah had remonstrated so strongly against the step, and had shown such desire to keep Phil under her roof as long as he should need one, that Mrs. Blake had yielded the point, and Phil himself had asked to be allowed to stay at Stony Brook Farm. "I'd love to go up there," he said a little wistfully, " but I think I'd better

Into the Sunset. 141

stay with Mrs Keturah, because she hasn't any boy but me and Jim, and you've got Carl and Carola. And I love Stony Brook Farm now, and I've got used to looking at that old apple-tree that looks like an ogre, and I guess I'd better stay, thank you."

The chief reason that Mrs. Blake had wanted to take Phil home with her had been that she was preparing him for his First Communion.

It had been arranged that by and by, just before he went away, the priest should come over from North Branscome, and give the little boy a First Communion that should also be a Viaticum. And Phil was such a thoughtful child, so wise beyond his years, taught as he was by poverty and suffering, that there was no difficulty in instructing him for this great day, nor any necessity for telling him why it must be. For, though no one had ever told him that he was not going to recover, Phil perfectly understood that he was to be one of those favored children whom Our Lord allows to leave earth and its hardships, to be just as happy as they can be forever.

"Just see how Rags sits and watches me," said Phil one day to Mrs. Blake. "He will hardly go away to eat. He knows, doesn't he?"

"Yes, I really think he does," said Mrs. Blake.

"Would it be wicked for me to ask Our Lord when I make my First Communion to give a nice home to Rags, because I mean to ask Him to take care of Jim?" asked Phil.

"No, dear; I think Our Lord was so loving when He was a little boy that He must have been fond of all the good little dogs and cats and birds and lambs in Nazareth," said Mrs. Blake. "But, dear little Phil boy, don't give another anxious thought to either Jim or Rags. I will look after them both; they shall come straight to me, and I will take them to New York this winter. Jim shall go to school with Carl, and Rags shall be Carola's especial charge."

"Oh!" cried Phil, looking so happy that it made Mrs. Blake rejoice. "Now I'm so glad I feel as if I wasn't big enough to be as glad as I feel. Please let me hug you." And Mrs. Blake did as she was requested.

It was the middle of September, and fiercely warm, with the dry heat that comes when summer should be over. There was a drought, and the dust made Phil cough, and brought on the hemorrhages more frequently, which, with the heat, so sapped his strength that Mrs. Blake said aloud, as she and Miss Keturah fanned him: "I think it would better be to-morrow."

"What say?" asked Miss Keturah.

"I did not know that I spoke aloud," said Mrs. Blake. "I think, if you please, Miss

Flint, I'll send for Father Woods to-morrow for the ceremony of which I told you."

"Do you think so?" said Miss Keturah, with a startled glance at Phil lying pale and quiet on his pillow. "Very well."

"I'll come down in the morning when Matt goes over to fetch the priest; and Carl and Carola would like to be here. I'll bring whatever is necessary, except a little table, and this one will be exactly right."

"Would there be any objections to me and Ella May being present?" asked Miss Keturah awkwardly. "I never did take kindly to Roman Catholics, and never thought to see a priest under my father's roof, but I must say I feel very different than I did towards 'em."

"Another good result of these children coming here," thought Mrs. Blake, but only said: "Not the slightest objection in the world, Miss Flint, if you won't mind kneeling when we do."

A dark cloud came rolling up in the west, and Mrs. Blake rose to go. "Asleep, Phil, dear?" she asked, stroking the child's forehead. He shook his head. "To-morrow, dear, you shall make your First Communion."

Phil opened his eyes, and smiled contentedly, but was too weak to say more than: "I'm glad, Mamma Blake. Good-night," in a faint whisper.

A thunder-shower in the night had cooled and enlivened the air, and when Mrs. Blake came she found Phil brighter. As he was too weak to fast, this First Communion was to be a Viaticum; but that would not take one jot from its joyousness to Phil had he realized it fully, nor would Mrs. Blake allow any sorrow in the hearts of the other children which she could banish. "It is not sad to die when one is good," she had told them, and she tried very hard to make them realize this.

The room was full of the sweetest and brightest flowers to be found in field and garden. The little table with its snowy cloth was garlanded with blossoms, and Phil lay waiting the solemn moment with such a happy face that no one else dared grieve; and though Jim's heart ached quietly, he managed to force a smile for Phil.

And presently the faint tinkle of a bell was heard, for Carl had gone with Matt to bring Father Woods to Stony Brook Farm, and was his acolyte. Jim lighted the candles, and all fell on their knees, even Miss Keturah, whose eyes were moist, and hard face soft with wonder and irrepressible awe.

"No sins since last week, Phil?" whispered the old priest.

"No, Father," said the child; and then amid perfect stillness Phil made his First Communion. For a few moments no one stirred, and then Mrs. Blake, still kneeling, sang, with a voice so sweet that Phil fancied he was already in heaven, "Jesus, the Very Thought of Thee," that sweetest of all hymns, and "Jesus,

Gentlest Saviour." One by one each of those present in turn kissed Phil's hallowed lips, and then all but Mrs. Blake and Jim crept softly away to let him rest; and thus happy little Phil received his first and last communion.

"Phil really seems better," cried Jim excitedly when Mrs. Blake came down two days later. She had not been well, and had not been to Stony Brook Farm the day before. "You don't know how much stronger he seems. Do you, oh! do you think he can be going to get well after all?"

Mrs. Blake shook her head. "I think he will be perfectly well and happy, Jim," she said. "I wish it weren't so hard for you to let the little fellow go." But when she saw Phil she was astonished; he looked so much brighter and stronger that she almost felt that he was to be lent to Jim for a little longer. "Good-night, Phil, my dear, and have a pleasant Sunday. Carl and Carola will be here to-morrow afternoon as usual, and I'll come on Monday. You look so well and bright that I think I shall have to tell Father Woods to send for you to straighten up the church-steeple, which you know is tipped a bit."

"Good-night," laughed Phil, kissing her. "When I see you again I'll be all well."

Carl and Carola found the same improvement in Phil when they went down to spend Sunday afternoon with him, which was the best substitute that could be obtained for the trips to the island which had been his chief happiness in Branscome. They told stories, and even played little quiet guessing-games, yet Phil's new strength did not flag. Ella May was allowed to join them, in spite of her aunt's objection to cheerful Sundays.

"Don't you tire Phil," said Miss Keturah, coming in, attracted by a merry peal of laughter.

"Why, Phil is lots better, Aunt Ket; he

doesn't seem to tire one mite," cried Ella May joyfully.

"I think mebbe you'd better say goodnight, though, for he hasn't got much strength to waste," said Miss Keturah.

"Yes, that's true; I hope we didn't stay too long. You ought to have told us to go before, Miss Flint," said Carola, rising.

"Oh, I guess you haven't done him any harm; he looks as if he'd had a real good time," said Miss Keturah with an indulgent smile that made her plain face attractive.

"Good-night, Carl," said Phil, putting out both hands. "Give my love to Matt and the horses. Good-night, Carola," he added, and as she went away he called her back. Throwing his arms around her, he kissed her, and laid his cheek lovingly on her dark curls. "I love you more than anybody but Jim," he whispered. "Good-night." He waved his hands to them as they ran down the walk, and smiled to Ella May, seeing them off on the door-step.

"I'll send one of the men for the cows, Jim," said Miss Keturah. "You stay with Phil awhile." "'Tain't likely they'll have many more Sunday nights," she thought.

"You're so good, I do love you lots now," said Phil. "Don't give me any supper; I've had so much jelly and things I'm not hungry."

"Well, I'll give you some milk and beef-tea after awhile," said Miss Keturah.

The sun was going down in splendor; long streamers of red and gold flamed up from the horizon, and reflected glory on Phil's little white face, and Jim's ruddy one laid close beside his on the pillow in the big chair where Phil most loved to lie.

"Sleepy, Phil?" asked Jim.

"A little, and I don't feel like saying a word. I love to sit and look at that, and know I've got you, Jim," Phil answered in a whisper.

Gradually the bright streamers changed to purple clouds with golden edges, and these faded into soft gray, and the stars began to come out; but Jim dared not move, for fear of disturbing Phil, though his arm ached from being so long in one position. Miss Keturah came in later with Phil's beef-tea, and aroused Jim from a nap into which he was falling. "Sh! don't wake up Phil; he's been asleep ever so long," he murmured.

Miss Keturah came softly and touched Phil's hand, felt him quickly from head to feet, and then, with a gentleness of which no one could have dreamed her capable, drew Jim's arm away, and laid her hand on the boy's shoulder. "I couldn't wake him," she said. "Jim, no one will ever wake him."

It was true. The gates which he had spoken of to Miss Keturah, that swung wide at sunset, had swung open noiselessly that night, and, while the two brothers had been watching the glory, little Phil had slipped through the gates into heaven.

CHAPTER XI.

GOOD-BY, JIM.

THE frail little body which Phil no longer needed was laid away under the big shade-trees in the small Catholic cemetery in North Branscome, and Jim and Rags had gone from Stony Brook Farm to the house on the hill. Ella May went back to her home, and the summer, with its joys and sorrows, was over.

Ella May surprised every one when the time came for her departure. She came up the hill one night as Jim and Carl and Carola were sitting on the piazza, talking soberly of little Phil.

"I came to say good-by," she said. "You needn't hate me, Jim; I have been mean and bad to you, and I've been a mean sort of girl anyhow; but I'm sorry, if you want to know it, and I'm not going to be bad any more; I'm going to try to be good and unselfish and lovely like Phil, and I see it's no matter how little or no consequence you are, if you're sweet and lovely like that you can't help making people happy. And I never thought anything about lots of things till I saw how patient and beautiful Phil was. And it ain't likely I'm going to forget how mean I was to him, and how if I hadn't been so ugly about finding out your island Phil might have been here now. And I guess I'll remember all my days how the dear little fellow pulled me out, and died because he did it. But Phil forgave me, and didn't seem to even remember it afterwards; so I think you might forgive me a little, Jim."

Ella May poured out this long speech, with flushed cheeks and quivering voice, so fast that no one could stop her; but as soon as she paused, Jim sprang up.

"Don't say any more, Ella May," he said. "I guess it's been hard on you. While Phil was sick I didn't feel as though I could ever get over what you did, but I feel different now he's—now. So I'll forgive you, and I hope you won't worry over what happened. The doctor says Phil was too frail a little fellow to grow up to be a man anyway. Good-by, and don't fret over things."

"Now who could have thought that she had it in her? exclaimed Carl as Ella May disappeared down the road.

"And isn't it beautiful that dear Phil did her so much good?" said Carola, who was much touched by what she had heard and seen.

Mrs. Blake came out at this moment, and the wonderful story of Ella May's visit was told her. "You won't say that you are sorry that you ever saw Branscome when you think of all that this summer has accomplished, Jim," she said. "There is dear little

Phil happy and safe forever, and Ella May taught how beautiful such a simple, holy little soul as his is, and you and Rags are not to have any more homeless and friendless days, but are to be just as safe and happy as kings—or as I can make you."

Jim managed to give her a smile that was more cheerful than any his lips had worn since the night that Phil had left him.

"You are so good to me, but I don't feel as though I ought to let you look after me," he said gratefully. "You know I am well and strong, and I ought to earn my own living."

"Thirteen is such a great age, Jim," said Mrs. Blake, smiling. "But you know we can't even question what you are to do; Phil and I decided that while he was sick; and even if you are no consequence, just think of poor little Rags! Seriously, Jim, I do not think you will be the worse for a few years of hard study, and then you can 'earn your own living,' as you say, and I hope may do a little more than that."

And, then one of those wonderful things happened that would seem unlikely in a story, and yet do happen often in real life. Matt drove up from the village, and stopped to give Mrs. Blake her letters. One among them in a business envelope she took up first, and exclaimed wonderingly: "Why, Jim, this is for you."

"For me? Oh, I guess not; I haven't any friends to write me," said Jim.

"For you," repeated Mrs. Blake. "'Master James Upper,' plain enough, and postmarked 'Washington.'"

Jim took the letter, opened it, and began reading it with a puzzled face. "Why, what in the world——" he muttered. "Oh! Mrs. Blake, look here. This man says he read in the New York *Cyclone* about Phil rescuing Ella May, and how we tramped here from New York. He says our name is so peculiar that he wonders if we can be the children of his sister, who married a man named Upper, and he tells me to write him, and he signs his name 'James Whiting.' Now my mother's name was Whiting, and you know I told you she was always trying to find her brother James, and never could."

"Does this man tell you anything about himself to help you decide whether or not he really is your uncle?" asked Mrs. Blake, looking excited, while the children listened in mute amazement to this wonderful thing that was happening.

"Why, yes," said Jim, turning the letter over and over in a dazed way, as if he were not quite sure of what it might still be capable. "I thought I told you. He says his sister was Mary, and his father's name was John, and those are my mother's and grandfather's names, and he tells me some other things— oh! yes; he's my uncle all right enough."

"But, Jim——" Mrs. Blake began. "Well,

there's no use in speculating; I suppose we shall have to wait to learn what sort of man he is, and if he means to help you on in the world, and all these important items."

"Oh! he says he's a rich man, and he hasn't any son, only one girl, for the rest died, and he wants to educate me if I really am his nephew. Here, you read it," and Jim offered the letter to Mrs. Blake with a look on his face like a person walking in his sleep.

Mrs. Blake read and then laid the pages down, feeling joy in the possibility of good fortune having come to Jim, and anxiety as to what this new influence on his life might bring forth.

"You must answer at once, Jim," she said at last, "and we will ask Mr. Blake to take measures to learn what sort of man this new uncle of yours is, and then if it is all right—but we will wait to see what are the results of these first steps."

Jim replied to the letter from Washington

that night, and Mr. Blake sent in the same mail a request to his lawyers to gather through the Washington branch of their firm all information regarding Mr. James Whiting, of the given number and street, which they could obtain.

The children could hardly wait for the reply, and no better help for Jim to bear his sorrow in the loss of Phil could have been devised than was found in this new interest. They speculated on the possible and impossible appearance of Mr. Whiting, on his wealth, on what he would do for Jim, and they vainly strove to reconcile themselves to the fact that if it all turned out as they must hope it would Jim would go to Washington to live, instead of going with them to New York.

At last came the letter from Mr. Whiting, and Jim's hands trembled as he tried to open it and learn what would be his fate.

"My dear Nephew," it began, and Carola, looking over Jim's shoulder, gasped. "There is no doubt that you are the son of my only sister, Mary Whiting, and her husband, Philip Upper. It seemed impossible to me that the combination of names which I saw in the newspaper could be a mere coincidence. Since you are my sister's boy, I take great pleasure in telling you that my home is yours, and would be were you not left in such sore need of a home. I will do for you everything that I would have done for my own boy had he lived; and if you prove the boy that I have no doubt you are, you shall take his place in every way. I am ready to go to Branscome to fetch you home to Washington on any day when you are ready to come to me. I am very grateful to the kind friends whom you have found in that place, and shall feel honored to take their hand and thank them personally. Do not think, my dear boy, that I am unsympathetic in the loss of the dear child whose brave unselfishness, as recorded in the paper, was the means in God's providence of bringing us together. There would have been enough love and welcome for him as well as you, but I have lived long enough in this world to know that it were not kind to wish him to stay in it, and we must try to comfort each other in the loss of my boy and your Phil, and not be selfish in grudging them heaven. Write me on what day you will be ready to come to

"Your affectionate uncle,
"JAMES WHITING."

"We hardly need to be told what kind of a man he is after such a simple, kind letter as that is," said Mrs. Blake when she read it. "I am sure he is good and true. Suppose we let your uncle come here next week on Tuesday? He can stay overnight, and then on Wednesday we will all go away together.

Mr. Blake brought a letter that night from his lawyers which told them the best things of Mr. Whiting as a man, and that he was said to be very wealthy. It was with unalloyed pleasure in the good fortune that had come to the boy whom they had all learned to love and respect for his honest truth and loving heart that the Blakes saw him write the letter that told his uncle he should be ready to go to his new home in the following week. That is, only the elder Blakes felt pleasure; Carl and Carola could hardly bring themselves to the necessary pitch of generosity to be glad to give Jim up, and Jim himself cared so little for the prospect of having all the best things of the world for his own that he looked very sober at the thought of the coming parting.

"Only think, only think," cried Carola over and over again, "if that young man had not come in that day when we took tea at Miss Flint's, and had not written about Phil in *The Cyclone*, you would never have found your uncle; and it's all just like a story."

"It will not be a real parting," said Mrs.

Blake. "I am sure your uncle will let you visit us in New York, and perhaps come for the summer vacations to Branscome."

"And if he doesn't like dogs, we'll take care of Rags," added Carl, who would not have objected to this arrangement.

Carola crept up to Jim, and, holding her curls away from her face, stooped to whisper to him: "It isn't as though you left Phil's grave here alone, Jim. We shall be here every summer, and each Sunday I'll cover it with flowers, and say a prayer for you."

Jim looked up into the soft dark eyes, and for the first time fully realized why gentle Carola always touched the very thought nearest the heart, and why little Phil had said he loved her best of all.

"Thank you, Carola," he said simply, but from that moment Jim too began to "love her best of all."

Mr. Whiting came—a big, silent man, with a grave, kindly manner, a firm clasp of hand, and a full, strong voice. Every one in the big house on the hill liked him from the first moment that he spoke, even the children and Rags, who were inclined to be critical for Jim's sake.

"Take Rags? By all means," said Mr. Whiting when Jim hinted his desire to know the true-hearted little beast's fate. "Rags is another nephew, you know." And Carola's heart was entirely his after that delightful speech.

After tea Jim took Mr. Whiting to see Phil's grave, and they came home from that long walk with perfect understanding of one another. The train left early in the morning, but Miss Keturah and Seth Peters were at the station to see them off.

Miss Keturah brought cookies and doughnuts and big "pound sweetings" from the orchard, and wrung Jim's hand at parting till it ached. This was her way of expressing regret for her many unjust and unkind acts in the past, for which she could never have begged pardon in words.

Seth Peters pressed a big bunch of fragrant herbs and the brilliant blossoms of the autumn into Jim's hand.

"He loved 'em," he said. "I want you should know I'm going to look after him, and keep sweet-smelling things over him as long as there are any to be found."

The train moved out of the station, and as it turned the curve of the road they saw the spire of the North Branscome church with its little golden cross gleaming in the bright October sunshine.

"Pray for me, Phil," whispered Jim. The intervening hill shut out the church again from sight, and the train bore Jim onward into his new life.

BOOKS OF DOCTRINE, INSTRUCTION, DEVOTION, MEDITATION, BIOGRAPHY, NOVELS, JUVENILES, ETC.

PUBLISHED BY
BENZIGER BROTHERS

NEW YORK   CINCINNATI   CHICAGO
36-38 BARCLAY ST.   429 MAIN ST.   205-207 W. WASHINGTON ST.

Books not marked *net* will be sent postpaid on receipt of the advertised price. Where books are marked *net* ten per cent. must be added for postage. Thus a book advertised at *net* $1.00 will be sent postpaid on receipt of $1.10.

I. INSTRUCTION, DOCTRINE, APOLOGETICS, CONTROVERSY, EDUCATIONAL

AMERICAN PRIEST, THE. SCHMIDT. *net*, $1.50.
ANECDOTES AND EXAMPLES ILLUSTRATING THE CATHOLIC CATECHISM. SPIRAGO. *net*, $2.75.
ART OF PROFITING BY OUR FAULTS. TISSOT. *net*, $0.75.
BOY GUIDANCE. KILIAN, O.M. Cap *net*, $2.00.
CATECHISM EXPLAINED, THE. SPIRAGO-CLARKE. *net*, $3.75.
CATECHISM OF THE VOWS FOR THE USE OF RELIGIOUS. COTEL, S.J. *net*, $0.75.
CATECHIST AND THE CATECHUMEN, THE. WEIGAND. *net*, $1.50.
CATHOLIC AMERICAN, THE. SCHMIDT. *net*, $0.85.
CATHOLIC BELIEF. FAÀ DI BRUNO. Paper, $0.25; cloth, *net*, $0.85.
CATHOLIC CEREMONIES AND EXPLANATION OF THE ECCLESIASTICAL YEAR. DURAND. Paper, $0.25; cloth, *net*, $0.85.
CATHOLIC CUSTOMS AND SYMBOLS. HENRY, Litt.D. *net*, $1.90.
CATHOLIC NURSERY RHYMES. SISTER MARY GERTRUDE. Retail, $0.25.
CATHOLIC'S READY ANSWER, THE. HILL, S.J. *net*, $2.00.
CATHOLIC TEACHER'S COMPANION, THE. KIRSCH, O.M. Sp. Imitation leather, *net*, $2.75; real leather, $3.75.
CATHOLIC TEACHING FOR YOUNG AND OLD. WRAY. Paper, $0.25; cloth, *net*, $0.85.
CEREMONIAL FOR ALTAR BOYS. BRITT, O.S.B. *net*, $0.60
CHILD PREPARED FOR FIRST COMMUNION. ZULUETA. Paper, *$0.08.
CHRISTIAN APOLOGETICS. DEVIVIER-MESSMER. *net*, $3.50.
CHURCH AND THE PROBLEMS OF TODAY, THE. SCHMIDT. *net*, $0.85.
CORRECT THING FOR CATHOLICS. BUGG. *net*, $1.25.
DIVINE GRACE. WIRTH. *net*, $0.40.
EXPLANATION OF THE BALTIMORE CATECHISM. KINKEAD. *net*, $1.25.
EXPLANATION OF THE APOSTLES' CREED. ROLFUS. *net*, $0.85.
EXPLANATION OF THE COMMANDMENTS. ROLFUS. *net*, $0.85.
EXPLANATION OF GOSPELS AND OF CATHOLIC WORSHIP. LAMBERT-BRENNAN. Paper, $0.25; cloth, *net*, $0.85.
EXPLANATION OF THE MASS. COCHEM. *net*, $0.85.
EXPLANATION OF THE HOLY SACRAMENTS. ROLFUS. *net*, $0.85.
EXPLANATION OF THE PRAYERS AND CEREMONIES OF THE MASS. LASANCE. O.S.B. *net*, $0.85.
EXTREME UNCTION. Paper, $0.08.

1

FINGER OF GOD, THE. Brown, M.A. net, $1.75.
FOLLOWING OF CHRIST, THE. Plain edition. With reflections. $0.35.
FUNDAMENTALS OF THE RELIGIOUS LIFE. Schleuter, S.J. net, $0.50.
FUTURE LIFE, THE. Sasia, S.J. net, $3.00.
GENERAL CONFESSION MADE EASY. Konings, C.SS.R. Cloth, *$0.25.
GENTLEMAN, A. Egan. net, $0.85.
GIFT OF THE KING. By a Religious. net, $0.60.
GOFFINE'S DEVOUT INSTRUCTIONS ON THE EPISTLES AND GOSPELS FOR THE SUNDAYS AND HOLY-DAYS. net, $1.75.
HANDBOOK OF THE CHRISTIAN RELIGION. Wilmers, S.J. net, $2.50.
HINTS TO PREACHERS. Henry, Litt.D. net, $1.90.
HOME VIRTUES, THE. Doyle, S.J. net, $1.25.
HOME WORLD, THE. Doyle, S.J. Paper, $0.25; cloth, net, $1.25.
HOW TO MAKE THE MISSION. By a Dominican Father. Paper, *$0.12.
IDEALS OF ST. FRANCIS OF ASSISI, THE. Felder, O.M. Cap.-Bittle, O.M. Cap. net. $4.00.
INTRODUCTION TO A DEVOUT LIFE. St. Francis de Sales. net, $1.00.
LADY, A. Bugg. net. $1.25.
LAWS OF THE KING. By a Religious. net, $0.60.
LETTERS ON MARRIAGE. Spalding, S.J. net, $1.25.
LITTLE ALTAR BOY'S MANUAL. $0.50.
LITTLE FLOWER'S LOVE FOR HER PARENTS, THE. Sister M. Eleanore, C.S.C., Ph.D. net, $0.20.
LITTLE FLOWER'S LOVE FOR THE HOLY EUCHARIST, THE. Sister M. Eleanore, C.S.C., Ph.D. net, $0.20.
MANUAL OF SELF-KNOWLEDGE AND CHRISTIAN PERFECTION, A. Henry, C.SS.R. net, $0.44.

MANUAL OF THEOLOGY FOR THE LAITY. Geiermann, C.SS.R. Paper, *$0.45; cloth, net, $0.90.
MASS-SERVER'S CARD. Per doz., net, $0.50.
MIND, THE. Pyne, S.J. net, $2.00.
NARROW WAY, THE. Geiermann, C.SS.R. net, $0.52.
OUR FIRST COMMUNION. Rev. William R. Kelly. List, $0.28; to schools, $0.21.
OUR NUNS. Lord, S.J. Regular Edition, $1.75; De Luxe Edition, net, $3.00.
OUT TO WIN. Straight Talks to Boys on the Way to Manhood. Conroy, S.J. net, $1.50.
POETS AND PILGRIMS. Batgy. School Ed., net, $1.50; Decorative Ed., net, $1.90.
QUEEN'S FESTIVALS, THE. By a Religious. net, $0.60.
RELIGION HOUR: BOOK ONE. Hannan, D.D. List, $0.28; net to schools, $0.21.
RELIGIOUS STATE, THE. St. Alphonsus. net, $0.47.
SACRAMENTALS OF THE HOLY CATHOLIC CHURCH. Lambing. Paper, $0.25; cloth, net, $0.85.
SHORT CONFERENCES ON THE SACRED HEART. Brinkmeyer. net, $0.53.
SHORT COURSE IN CATHOLIC DOCTRINE. Paper, *$0.12.
SHORT STORIES ON CHRISTIAN DOCTRINE. net, $0.85.
SIMPLE COURSE OF RELIGION. Weigand. net, price to schools per 100, $4.00.
SIX ONE-ACT PLAYS. Lord, S.J. net, $1.75.
SOCIAL ORGANIZATION IN PARISHES. Garesché, S.J. net, $2.75.
SOCIAL PROBLEMS AND AGENCIES. Spalding, S.J. net, $2.50.
SOCIALISM: ITS THEORETICAL BASIS AND PRACTICAL APPLICATION. Cathrein-Gettelman. net, $2.75.
SODALITY CONFERENCES. Garesché, S.J. net, $2.75. First Series.
SODALITY CONFERENCES. Garesché, S.J. net, $2.75. Second Series.

SPIRITISM FACTS AND FRAUDS. BLACKMORE, S.J. net, $2.90.
SPIRITUAL PEPPER AND SALT. STANG. Paper, *$0.45; cloth, net, $0.90.
STORIES OF THE MIRACLES OF OUR LORD. By a Religious. net, $0.60.
SUNDAY-SCHOOL DIRECTOR'S GUIDE. SLOAN. net, $0.40.
SUNDAY-SCHOOL TEACHER'S GUIDE. SLOAN. net, $0.85.
TALKS TO BOYS. CONROY, S.J. Paper, $0.25.
TALKS TO NURSES: SPALDING, S.J. net, $1.50.
TALKS TO PARENTS. CONROY, S.J. net, $1.50.
TALKS WITH OUR DAUGHTERS, SISTER M. ELEANORE, PH.D. Cloth. net, $1.25, ooze leather, net, $2.00.
TALKS WITH TEACHERS. SISTER M. PAULA. net, $1.50.
TEACHER TELLS A STORY: BOOK ONE. HANNAN, D.D. list $2.00.
TRUE POLITENESS. DEMORE. net. $0.85.
VOCATIONS EXPLAINED. Cut flush, *$0.12.
WAY OF INTERIOR PEACE. LEHEN, S.J. net, $2.25.
WHAT THE CHURCH TEACHES. DRURY. Paper *$0.24; cloth, net, $0.45.
WONDERFUL SACRAMENTS, THE. DOYLE, S.J. net, paper, $0.25; cloth, net, $1.25.
WONDER DAYS, THE. TAGGART. net, $0.35.
WONDER GIFTS, THE. TAGGART. net, $0.35.
WONDER OFFERING, THE. TAGGART. net, $0.55.
WONDER STORY, THE. TAGGART. net, $0.35.

II. DEVOTION, MEDITATION, SPIRITUAL READING.
PRAYER-BOOKS

ABANDONMENT; or Absolute Surrender of Self to Divine Providence. CAUSSADE, S.J. net, $0.75.
ADORATION OF THE BLESSED SACRAMENT. TESNIERE. net, $0.85.
BLESSED SACRAMENT BOOK. Prayer-Book by FATHER LASANCE. Im. leather. $2.25.
BREAD OF LIFE, THE. WILLIAM. net, $1.35.
CATHOLIC GIRL'S GUIDE, THE. Prayer-Book by FATHER LASANCE. Seal grain cloth, stiff covers, red edges, $1.35. Im. leather, limp, red edges, $1.50; gold edges, $2.00. Real leather, limp, gold edges, $2.25.
COMMUNION DEVOTIONS FOR RELIGIOUS. SISTERS OF NOTRE DAME. Imitation leather, net, $2.75; leather, $3.75.
DEVOTIONS AND PRAYERS FOR THE SICK ROOM. KREBS. net, $0.85.
EARLY FRIENDS OF CHRIST, THE. CONROY, S.J. net, $1.75.
EPITOME OF THE PRIESTLY LIFE, AN. ARVISENET-O'SULLIVAN. net, $2.50.
EVER TIMELY THOUGHTS. GARESCHE, S.J. net, $0.90.
FAIREST FLOWER OF PARADISE. LEPICIER, O.S.M. net, $1.50.
FIRST SPIRITUAL AID TO THE SICK. MCGRATH. net, $0.30.
FOR FREQUENT COMMUNICANTS. ROCHE, S.J. Paper, *$0.12.
GO TO JOSEPH. LEPICIER, O.S.M. net, $1.50.
HELP FOR THE POOR SOULS. ACKERMANN, $0.45.
HER LITTLE WAY. CLARKE. net, $1.00.
HOLY HOUR, THE. KEILEY. 16mo, *$0.12.
HOLY HOUR OF ADORATION. STANG. net, $0.90.
HOLY SOULS BOOK. Reflections on Purgatory. A Complete Prayer-Book. By Rev. F. X. LASANCE. Imitation leather, round corners, red edges, $1.75; gold edges, $2.25; real leather, gold edges, $3.00.
HOLY VIATICUM OF LIFE AS OF DEATH. DEVER. net, $0.60.

IMITATION OF THE SACRED HEART. Arnoudt. net. $1.75.
JESUS CHRIST, THE KING OF OUR HEARTS. Lepicier, O.S.M. net, $1.50.
KEEP THE GATE. Williams, S.J. net, $1.50.
LET US PRAY. Lasance. Retail, $0.25.
LIFE'S LESSONS. Garesche, S.J. net, $0.90.
LITTLE COMMUNICANTS' PRAYER-BOOK. Sloan. $0.25.
LITTLE FLOWER AND THE BLESSED SACRAMENT, THE. Husslein, S.J. net, $0.50.
LITTLE MANUAL OF ST. ANTHONY. Lasance. net, $0.35.
LITTLE MANUAL OF ST. JOSEPH. Lings. net, $0.25.
LITTLE MANUAL OF ST. RITA. McGrath. $0.90.
LITTLE MASS BOOK, THE. Lynch. Paper, *$0.10.
LITTLE OFFICE OF THE BLESSED VIRGIN MARY. In Lat.-Eng. net, $1.50; in Latin only, net $1.25.
LITTLE OFFICE OF THE IMMACULATE CONCEPTION. Paper. *$0.08.
MANNA OF THE SOUL. Vestpocket Edition. A little Book of Prayer for Men and Women. By Rev. F. X. Lasance. Oblong, 32mo. $0.85.
MANNA OF THE SOUL. A Book of Prayer for Men and Women. By Rev. F. X. Lasance. Extra Large Type Edition, 544 pages, 16mo. $1.75.
MANNA OF THE SOUL. Prayer-Book by Rev. F. X. Lasance. Thin Edition. Im. leather. $1.25.
MANNA OF THE SOUL. Prayer-Book by Rev. F. X. Lasance. Thin Edition with Epistles and Gospels. $1.50.
MANUAL OF THE HOLY EUCHARIST. Lasance. Imitation leather, limp, red edges. net, $1.75.
MARY, HELP OF CHRISTIANS. Hammer, O.F.M. net $1.00.
MASS DEVOTIONS AND READINGS ON THE MASS. Lasance. Im. leather, limp, red edges. net, $1.75.

MASS FOR CHILDREN, THE. Kelly. list $0.28; net, $0.21.
MEDITATIONS FOR EVERY DAY IN THE YEAR ON THE LIFE OF OUR LORD. Vercruysse, S.J. 2 vols. net, $4.50.
MEDITATIONS FOR THE USE OF THE SECULAR CLERGY. Chaignon, S.J. 2 vols. net, $7.00.
MEDITATIONS ON THE SEVEN WORDS OF OUR LORD ON THE CROSS. Perraud. net, $1.00.
MEDITATIONS ON THE LIFE, THE TEACHING AND THE PASSION OF JESUS CHRIST. Ilg-Clarke. 2 vols. net, $5.00.
MEDITATIONS ON THE SUFFERINGS OF JESUS CHRIST. Perinaldo. net, $0.85.
MENDING THE NETS. MORNING-STAR SERIES II. Feely, S.J. net, $0.60.
MISSION REMEMBRANCE OF THE REDEMPTORIST FATHERS. Geiermann, C.SS.R. $0.90.
MOMENTS BEFORE THE TABERNACLE. Russell, S.J. net, $0.60.
MORE SHORT SPIRITUAL READINGS FOR MARY'S CHILDREN. Cecilia. net, $0.85.
MOST BELOVED WOMAN, THE. Garesche, S.J. net, $0.90.
MY GOD AND MY ALL. A Prayer-Book for Children. By Rev. F. X. Lasance. Black or white, cloth, square corners, white edges, retail, $0.35. Imit. leather, black or white, seal grain, gold edges, retail, $0.70. Persian Morocco, gold side and edges, retail, $1.25. Same, white leather, retail, $1.50. Celluloid, retail, $1.00; with Indulgence Cross, retail, $1.35.
MY PRAYER-BOOK. Happiness in Goodness. Reflections, Counsels, Prayers, and Devotions. By Rev. F. X. Lasance. 16mo. Seal grain cloth, stiff covers, $1.35. Imitation leather, limp, round corners, red edges, $1.50; gold edges, $2.00. Real leather, gold edges, $2.25.

MY PRAYER-BOOK. Extra Large Type Edition. By Rev. F. X. LASANCE. Seal grain cloth, stiff covers, square corners, red edges, $1.75. Imitation leather, round corners, red edges, $2.00. Imitation leather, round corners, gold edges, $2.75. American seal, limp, gold side, gold edges, $3.25.

MYSTERY OF LOVE, THE. LEPICIER, O.S.M. net, $1.50.

NEW MISSAL FOR EVERY DAY, THE. Complete Missal in English for Every Day in the Year. New 1924 Edition. With Introduction Notes, and a Book of Prayer. By Rev. F. X. LASANCE. Oblong, 32mo. Imitation leather. $2.75.

NEW MISSAL FOR EVERY DAY. (Student's Edition.) By Rev. F. X. LASANCE. Retail $1.75.

NEW TESTAMENT. 12mo edition. Large type. Cloth, net, $1.75; 32mo edition. Flexible, net, $0.45; cloth, net, $0.80; Amer. seal, net, $1.35.

NEW TESTAMENT AND PRAYER-BOOK COMBINED. net, $0.85.

NOVENA IN HONOR OF SAINT THERESE OF THE CHILD JESUS. COLEMAN, net, $0.15.

OFFICE OF HOLY WEEK, COMPLETE. Latin and English. Cut flush, net, $0.45; silk cloth, net, $0.60; Am. seal, red edges, net, $1.25.

OUR FAVORITE DEVOTIONS. LINGS. net, $1.00.

OUR FAVORITE NOVENAS. LINGS. net, $1.00.

OUR LADY BOOK. By Rev. F. X. LASANCE. Imitation leather, limp, round corners, red edges, $1.55. Morocco Grain, Imitation Leather, gold edges, $2.50. American Seal, limp, gold side, gold edges, $2.60. Rutland, limp, red under gold edges, $3.75. Turkey Morocco, limp, gold roll, red under gold edges, $4.75.

OUTLINE MEDITATIONS. CECILIA. net, $1.75.

PATHS OF GOODNESS, THE. GARESCHE, S.J. net, $0.90.

POCKET PRAYER-BOOK. Cloth. net, $0.45.

POLICEMEN'S AND FIREMEN'S COMPANION. McGRATH. $0.35.

PRAYER-BOOK FOR RELIGIOUS. LASANCE. 16mo. Imitation leather, limp, red edges, net, $2.50.

PRAYERS FOR OUR DEAD. McGRATH. Cloth, $0.35; imitation leather, $0.75.

PRISONER OF LOVE. Prayer-Book by FATHER LASANCE. Im. leather, limp, red edges, $2.00.

REFLECTIONS FOR RELIGIOUS. LASANCE. net, $2.50.

REJOICE IN THE LORD. Prayer-Book by FATHER LASANCE. $1.75.

ROSARY NOVENAS TO OUR LADY. LACEY. net, $0.15.

ROSARY, THE CROWN OF MARY. Dominican Father. 16mo, paper. *$0.12.

ROSE WREATH FOR THE CROWNING, A. REV. JOHN P. CLARKE. net, $1.00.

RULES OF LIFE FOR THE PASTOR OF SOULS. SLATER-RAUCH. net, $0.45.

SACRED HEART BOOK. Prayer-Book by FATHER LASANCE. Im. leather, limp, red edges, $1.75.

SECRET OF SANCTITY. CRASSET, S.J. net, $0.85.

SERAPHIC GUIDE, THE. $1.00

SHORT MEDITATIONS FOR EVERY DAY. LASAUSSE. net, $0.85.

SHORT VISITS TO THE BLESSED SACRAMENT. LASANCE. net, $0.35.

SOLDIERS' AND SAILORS' COMPANION. McGRATH. Vest-pocket shape, silk cloth or khaki. $0.35.

SOUVENIR OF THE NOVITIATE. TAYLOR. net, $0.85.

SPIRIT OF SACRIFICE, THE, AND THE LIFE OF SACRIFICE IN THE RELIGIOUS STATE. GIRAUD. net, $2.00.

SPIRITUAL CONSIDERATIONS. BUCKLER, O.P. net, $0.85.

SUNDAY MISSAL, THE. LASANCE, Im. leather, limp, red edges, $1.90.

TEACHINGS OF THE LITTLE FLOWER, THE. Garesché, S.J. net, $1.25.
THINGS IMMORTAL, THE. Garesché, S.J. net, $0.90.
THOUGHTS FOR TODAY. MORNING-STAR SERIES I. Feely, S.J. net, $0.60.
THOUGHTS ON THE RELIGIOUS LIFE. Lasance. Im. leather, limp, red edges, net, $2.50.
THY KINGDOM COME. SERIES I. Moffatt, S.J. net, $0.30.
THY KINGDOM COME. SERIES II. Moffatt, S.J. net, $0.30.
THY KINGDOM COME. SERIES III. Moffatt, S.J. net, $0.30.
THY KINGDOM COME. SERIES IV. Moffatt, S.J. net, $0.30.
TRUE SPOUSE OF CHRIST. Liguori. net, $1.75.
VALUES EVERLASTING, THE. Garesché, S.J. net, $0.90.
VENERATION OF THE BLESSED VIRGIN. Rohner-Brennan. net, $0.85.
VIGIL HOUR, THE. Ryan, S.J. Paper, *$0.12.
VISITS TO JESUS IN THE TABERNACLE. Lasance. Im. leather, limp, red edges, $2.00.
VISITS TO THE MOST HOLY SACRAMENT. Liguori. net, $0.90.
WAY OF THE CROSS. Paper. *$0.08.
WAY OF THE CROSS, THE. Very large-type edition. Method of St. Alphonsus Liguori. *$0.20.
WAY OF THE CROSS. Eucharistic method. *$0.15.
WAY OF THE CROSS. Method of St. Francis of Assisi. *$0.15.
WITH GOD. Prayer-Book by Father Lasance. Im. leather, limp, red edges, $2.00.
YEARNING FOR GOD. Williams, S.J. net, $1.50.
YOUNG MAN'S GUIDE, THE. Prayer-Book by Father Lasance. Seal grain cloth, stiff covers, red edges, $1.35. Im. leather, limp, red edges, $1.50; gold edges, $2.00.
YOUR INTERESTS ETERNAL. Garesché, S.J. net, $0.90.
YOUR NEIGHBOR AND YOU. Garesché, S.J. net, $0.90.
YOUR OWN HEART. Garesché, S.J. net, $0.90.
YOUR SOUL'S SALVATION. Garesché, S.J. net, $0.90.

III. THEOLOGY, LITURGY, HOLY SCRIPTURE, PHILOSOPHY, SCIENCE, CANON LAW

ALTAR PRAYERS. Edition A: English and Latin, net, $1.75. Edition B: German-English-Latin, net, $2.00.
ANNOUNCEMENT BOOK. 12mo. net, $2.50.
AUTOBIOGRAPHY OF AN OLD BREVIARY. Heuser, D.D. net, $1.75.
BAPTISMAL RITUAL. 12mo. net, $1.50.
BENEDICENDA. Schulte. net, $2.75.
BURIAL RITUAL. Cloth, net, $2.50; sheepskin, net, $3.75.
CHRIST'S TEACHING CONCERNING DIVORCE. Gigot. net, 1$0.67.
COMBINATION RECORD FOR SMALL PARISHES. net, $8.00.
COMPENDIUM SACRÆ LITURGIÆ. Wapelhorst, O.F.M. net, $36.00.
GENERAL INTRODUCTION TO THE STUDY OF THE HOLY SCRIPTURES. Gigot. net, 1$4.00.
GENERAL INTRODUCTION TO THE STUDY OF THE HOLY SCRIPTURES. Abridged edition. Gigot. net, 1$2.75.
HOLY BIBLE, THE. Large type, handy size. Cloth, $2.50.
HYMNS OF THE BREVIARY AND MISSAL, THE. Britt, O.S.B. net, $3.00.
JESUS LIVING IN THE PRIEST. Millet, S.J.-Byrne. net, $3.25.
LIBER STATUS ANIMARUM, or Parish Census Book. Large edition, size, 14x10 inches. 100 Families. 200 pp., half leather, net, $7.00; 200 Families, 400 pp., half leather, net, $8.00; Pocket Edition. net, $0.50.

MARRIAGE LEGISLATION IN THE NEW CODE. AYRINHAC, S.S. *net*, $2.50.
MARRIAGE RITUAL. Cloth, gilt edges, *net*, $2.50; sheepskin, gilt edges, *net*, $3.75.
MISSALE ROMANUM. Benziger Brothers' Authorized Vatican Edition. Black or Red Amer. morocco, gold edges, *net*, $15.00; Red Amer. morocco, gold stamping and edges, *net*, $17.50. Red finest quality morocco, red under gold edges, *net*, $22.00.
MORAL PRINCIPLES AND MEDICAL PRACTICE. Coppens, S.J.-Spalding, S.J. *net*, $2.50.
OUTLINES OF JEWISH HISTORY. Gigot, D.D. *net*, $2.75.
OUTLINES OF NEW TESTAMENT HISTORY. Gigot. *net*, 1 $2.75.
PASTORAL THEOLOGY. Stang. *net*, 1 $2.25.
PENAL LEGISLATION IN THE NEW CODE OF CANON LAW. AYRINHAC, S.S. *net*, $3.00.

PEW COLLECTION AND RECEIPT BOOK. Indexed. Full inches, *net*, $3.00.
PREPARATION FOR MARRIAGE. McHugh, O.P. *net*, $0.40.
RECORD OF BAPTISMS. 200 pages, 700 entries, *net*, $7.00. 400 pages. 1400 entries, *net*, $10.00. 600 pages, 2100 entries, *net*, $12.00.
RECORD OF CONFIRMATIONS. *net*, $6.00.
RECORD OF FIRST COMMUNIONS. *net*, $6.00.
RECORD OF INTERMENTS. *net*, $6.00.
RECORD OF MARRIAGES. Size 14x10 inches. 200 pages, 700 entries, *net*, $7.00. 400 pages, 1400 entries, *net* $10.00. 600 pages, 2100 entries. *net*, $12.00.
RITUALE COMPENDIOSUM. Cloth, *net*, $1.25; seal, *net*, $2.00.
SPECIAL INTRODUCTION TO THE STUDY OF THE OLD TESTAMENT. Gigot. Part I, *net*, 1 $2.75. Part II, *net*, 1 $3.25.
TEXTUAL CONCORDANCE OF THE HOLY SCRIPTURES. Williams. *net*, $5.75.

IV. SERMONS

EIGHT-MINUTE SERMONS. Demouy. 2 vols., *net*, $4.00.
FUNERAL SERMONS. Wirth, O.S.B. *net*, $3.00.
HINTS TO PREACHERS. Henry, Litt.D. *net*, $1.90.
POPULAR SERMONS ON THE CATECHISM. Bamberg-Thurston, S.J. 3 vols., *net*, $7.50.
SERMONS. Canon Sheehan. *net*, $3.00.
SERMONS. Whelan, O.S.A. *net*, $2.00.

SERMONS FOR THE SUNDAYS AND CHIEF FESTIVALS OF THE ECCLESIASTICAL YEAR. Pottgiesser, S.J. 2 vols., *net*, $5.00.
SODALITY CONFERENCES. Garesché, S.J. *net*, $2.75. First Series.
SODALITY CONFERENCES. Garesché, S.J. *net*, $2.75. Second Series.
THREE-MINUTE HOMILIES. McDonough. *net*, $2.00.

V. HISTORY, BIOGRAPHY, HAGIOLOGY, TRAVEL

CHILD'S LIFE OF ST. JOAN OF ARC. Mannix. *net*, $1.50.
HISTORY OF THE CATHOLIC CHURCH. Brueck. 2 vols., *net*, $5.50.
HISTORY OF THE PROTESTANT REFORMATION. Cobbett-Gasquet. *net*, $0.85.
HISTORY OF THE MASS. O'Brien. *net*, $2.00.
IDEALS OF ST. FRANCIS OF ASSISI, THE. Felder, O.M. Cap. *net*, $4.00.

ILLUSTRATED LIVES OF PATRON SAINTS FOR BOYS. Mannix. *net*, $1.00.
ILLUSTRATED LIVES OF PATRON SAINTS FOR GIRLS. Mannix. *net*, $1.00.
IN THE WORKSHOP OF ST. JOSEPH. Heuser, D.D. *net*, $2.75.
LIFE OF ST. MARGARET MARY ALACOQUE. Illustrated. Bougaud. *net*, $1.94.

LIFE OF CHRIST. Businger-Brennan. Illustrated. Half morocco, gilt edges, net, $15.00.
LIFE OF CHRIST. Illustrated. Businger-Mullett. net, $1.00.
LIFE OF CHRIST. Cochem. net, $0.85.
LIFE OF ST. IGNATIUS LOYOLA. Genelli, S.J. net, $0.56.
LIFE OF MADEMOISELLE LE GRAS. net, $0.85.
LIFE OF THE BLESSED VIRGIN. Rohner. net, $0.85.
LITTLE LIVES OF THE SAINTS FOR CHILDREN. Berthold. net, $0.75.
LITTLE PICTORIAL LIVES OF THE SAINTS. With 400 illustrations. net, $2.00.
LIVES OF THE SAINTS. Butler. Paper, $0.25; cloth, net, $0.85.
LOURDES. Clarke, S.J. net, $0.85.
MARY THE QUEEN. By a Religious. net, $0.60.
MILL TOWN PASTOR, A. Conroy, S.J. net, $1.75.
OUR NUNS. Lord, S.J. Regular Edition, $1.75; DeLuxe Edition, net, $3.00.
OUR OWN ST. RITA. Corcoran. O.S.A. net, $1.50.
PASSIONISTS, THE. Ward, C.P. net, $4.00.
PATRON SAINTS FOR CATHOLIC YOUTH. By M. E. Mannix. Each life separately in attractive colored paper cover with illustration on front cover. Each 10 cents postpaid; per 25 copies, assorted, net, $1.75; per 100 copies, assorted, net, $6.75. Sold only in packages containing 5 copies of one title.
   For Boys: St. Joseph; St. Aloysius; St. Anthony; St. Bernard; St. Martin; St. Michael; St. Francis Xavier; St. Patrick; St. Charles; St. Philip.
   The above can be had bound in 1 volume, cloth, net, $1.00.
   For Girls: St. Ann; St. Agnes; St. Teresa; St. Rose of Lima; St. Cecilia; St. Helena; St. Bridget; St. Catherine; St. Elizabeth; St. Margaret.
   The above can be had bound in 1 volume, cloth, net, $1.00.
PICTORIAL LIVES OF THE SAINTS. With nearly 400 illustrations and over 600 pages, net, $5.00.
POPULAR LIFE OF ST. TERESA. L'Abbé Joseph. net, $0.85.
ROMA. Pagan Subterranean and Modern Rome in Word and Picture. By Rev. Albert Kuhn, O.S.B., D.D. Preface by Cardinal Gibbons. 617 pages, 744 illustrations. 48 full-page inserts, 3 plans of Rome in colors. 8½x12 inches. Red im. leather, gold side. net, $12.00.
ROMAN CURIA AS IT NOW EXISTS. Martin, S.J. net, $0.80.
ST. ANTHONY. Ward. net, $0.85.
ST. JOAN OF ARC. Lynch, S.J. Illustrated. net, $2.75.
ST. JOHN BERCHMANS. Delmave, S.J.-Semple, S.J. net, $1.50.
SHORT LIFE OF CHRIST, A. McDonough. net, $0.15.
SHORT LIVES OF THE SAINTS. Donnelly. net, $0.90.
STORY OF JESUS, THE. Mulholland. net, $0.50.
STORY OF THE DIVINE CHILD. Told for Children. Lings. net, $0.60.
STORY OF THE ACTS OF THE APOSTLES. Lynch, S.J. Illustrated. net, $2.75.
STORY OF THE LITTLE FLOWER, THE. Lord, S.J. Retail, $0.15 net to Priests and Religious, $0.10.
WHISPERINGS OF THE CARIBBEAN. Williams, S.J. net, $2.00.
WONDER STORY, THE. Taggart. Illustrated Board covers, net, $0.35; per 100, $31.50. Also an edition in French and Polish at same prices.

VI. JUVENILES

FATHER FINN'S BOOKS. Each, net, $1.00.
SUNSHINE AND FRECKLES.

LORD BOUNTIFUL.
ON THE RUN.
BOBBY IN MOVIELAND.

FACING DANGER.
HIS LUCKIEST YEAR. A Sequel to "Lucky Bob."
LUCKY BOB.
PERCY WYNN; OR, MAKING A BOY OF HIM.
TOM PLAYFAIR; OR, MAKING A STRAT.
CLAUDE LIGHTFOOT; OR, HOW THE PROBLEM WAS SOLVED.
HARRY DEE; OR, WORKING IT OUT.
ETHELRED PRESTON; OR, THE ADVENTURES OF A NEW COMER.
THE BEST FOOT FORWARD; AND OTHER STORIES.
"BUT THY LOVE AND THY GRACE."
CUPID OF CAMPION.
THAT FOOTBALL GAME, AND WHAT CAME OF IT.
THE FAIRY OF THE SNOWS.
THAT OFFICE BOY.
HIS FIRST AND LAST APPEARANCE.
MOSTLY BOYS. SHORT STORIES.

FATHER SPALDING'S BOOKS. Each, net, $1.00.
STRANDED ON LONG BAR.
IN THE WILDS OF THE CANYON.
SIGNALS FROM THE BAY TREE.
HELD IN THE EVERGLADES.
AT THE FOOT OF THE SANDHILLS.
THE CAVE BY THE BEECH FORK.
THE SHERIFF OF THE BEECH FORK.
THE CAMP BY COPPER RIVER.
THE RACE FOR COPPER ISLAND.
THE MARKS OF THE BEAR CLAWS.
THE OLD MILL ON THE WITHROSE.
THE SUGAR CAMP AND AFTER.

ADVENTURE WITH THE APACHES. Ferry. net, $0.60.
ALTHEA. Niedlinger. net, $0.85.
AS GOLD IN THE FURNACE. Copus, S.J. net, $0.85.
AS TRUE AS GOLD. Mannix. net, $0.60.
AT THE FOOT OF THE SANDHILLS. Spalding, S.J. net, $1.00.
AWAKENING OF EDITH, THE. Illustrated. Specking. net, $1.50.
BERKLEYS, THE. Wight. net, $0.60.
BEST FOOT FORWARD, THE. Finn, S.J. net, $1.00.
BETWEEN FRIENDS. Aumerle. net, $0.85
BISTOURI. Melandri net, $0.60.
BLISSYLVANIA POST-OFFICE. Taggart. net, $0.60.
BOBBY IN MOVIELAND. Finn, S.J. net, $1.00.
BOB O'LINK. Waggaman. net, $0.60.
BROWNIE AND I. Aumerle. net, $0.85.
BUNT AND BILL. Mulholland. net, $0.60.
"BUT THY LOVE AND THY GRACE." Finn, S.J. net, $1.00.
BY BRANSCOME RIVER. Taggart. net, $0.60.
CAMP BY COPPER RIVER. Spalding, S.J. net, $1.00.
CAPTAIN TED. Waggaman. net, $1.25.
CAVE BY THE BEECH FORK. Spalding, S.J. net, $1.00.
CHILDREN OF CUPA. Mannix. net, $0.60.
CHILDREN OF THE LOG CABIN. Delamare. net, $0.85.
CLARE LORAINE. "Lee." net, $0.85.
CLAUDE LIGHTFOOT. Finn, S.J. net, $1.00.
COBRA ISLAND. Boyton, S.J. net, $1.25.
CUPA REVISITED. Mannix. net, $0.60.
CUPID OF CAMPION. Finn, S.J. net, $1.00.
DADDY DAN. Waggaman. net, $0.60.
DAN'S BEST ENEMY. Holland, S.J. net, $1.25.
DEAR FRIENDS. Niedlinger. net, $0.85.
DEAREST GIRL, THE. Taggart. net, $1.50.
DIMPLING'S SUCCESS. Mulholland. net, $0.60.
ETHELRED PRESTON. Finn, S.J. net, $1.00.

EVERY-DAY GIRL, AN. Crowley. net, $0.60.
FACING DANGER. Finn, S.J. net, $1.00.
FAIRY OF THE SNOWS. Finn, S.J. net, $1.00.
FINDING OF TONY. Waggaman. net, $1.25.
FIVE BIRDS IN A NEST. Delamare. net, $0.85.
FOR THE WHITE ROSE. Hinkson. net, $0.60.
FRED'S LITTLE DAUGHTER. Smith. net, $0.60.
FREDDY CARR'S ADVENTURES. Garrold, S.J. net, $0.85.
FREDDY CARR AND HIS FRIENDS. Garrold, S.J. net, $0.85.
GOLDEN LILY, THE. Hinkson. net, $0.60.
GREAT CAPTAIN, THE. Hinkson. net, $0.60.
HALDEMAN CHILDREN, THE. Mannix. net, $0.60.
HARMONY FLATS. Whitmire. net, $0.85.
HARRY DEE. Finn, S.J. net, $1.00.
HARRY RUSSELL. Copus, S.J. net, $0.85.
HEIR OF DREAMS, AN. O'Malley. net, $0.60.
HELD IN THE EVERGLADES. Spalding, S.J. net, $1.00.
HIS FIRST AND LAST APPEARANCE. Finn, S.J. net, $1.00.
HIS LUCKIEST YEAR. Finn, S.J. net, $1.00.
HOI-AH! McDonald. net, $1.25
HOSTAGE OF WAR, A. Bonesteel. net, $0.60.
HOW THEY WORKED THEIR WAY. Egan. net, $0.85.
IN QUEST OF ADVENTURE. Mannix. net, $0.60.
IN QUEST OF THE GOLDEN CHEST. Barton. net, $0.85.
IN THE WILDS OF THE CANYON. Spalding, S.J. net, $1.00.
JACK. By a Religious, H.C.J. net, $0.60.
JACK-O'LANTERN. Waggaman. net, $0.60.
JACK HILDRETH ON THE NILE. Taggart. net, $0.85.
JUNIORS OF ST. BEDE'S. Bryson. net, $0.85.

KLONDIKE PICNIC, A. Donnelly. net, $0.85.
LAST LAP, THE. McGrath, S.J. net, $1.50.
LITTLE APOSTLE ON CRUTCHES. Delamare. net, $0.60.
LITTLE GIRL FROM BACK EAST. Roberts. net, $0.60.
LITTLE LADY OF THE HALL. Ryeman. net, $0.60.
LITTLE MARSHALLS AT THE LAKE. Nixon-Roulet. net, $0.85.
LITTLE MISSY. Waggaman. net, $0.60.
LOYAL BLUE AND ROYAL SCARLET. Taggart. net, $1.25.
LORD BOUNTIFUL. Finn, S.J. net, $1.00.
LUCKY BOB. Finn, S.J. net, $1.00.
MADCAP SET AT ST. ANNE'S. Brunowe. net, $0.60.
MAD KNIGHT, THE. Schaching. net, $0.60.
MAKING OF MORTLAKE. Copus, S.J. net, $0.85.
MAN FROM NOWHERE. Sadlier. net, $0.85.
MARKS OF THE BEAR CLAWS. Spalding, S.J. net, $1.00.
MARTHA JANE. Specking. net, $1.50.
MARY ROSE AT BOARDING SCHOOL. Wibbies. net, $1.00.
MARY ROSE KEEPS HOUSE. Wibbies. net, $1.00.
MARY ROSE SOPHOMORE. Wibbies. net, $1.00.
MARY TRACY'S FORTUNE. Sadlier. net, $0.60.
MILLY AVELING. Smith. net, $0.85.
MIRALDA. Johnson. net, $0.60.
MOSTLY BOYS. Finn, S.J. net, $1.00.
MYSTERIOUS DOORWAY. Sadlier. net, $0.60.
MYSTERY OF CLEVERLY. Barton. net, $0.85.
MYSTERY OF HORNBY HALL. Sadlier. net, $0.85.
NAN NOBODY. Waggaman. net, $0.60.
NED RIEDER. Wehs. net, $0.85.
NEW SCHOLAR AT ST. ANNE'S. Brunowe. net, $0.85.
OLD CHARLMONT'S SEED BED. Smith. net, $0.60.

www.ingramcontent.com/pod-product-compliance
Lightning Source LLC
Chambersburg PA
CBHW020302170426
43202CB00008B/462